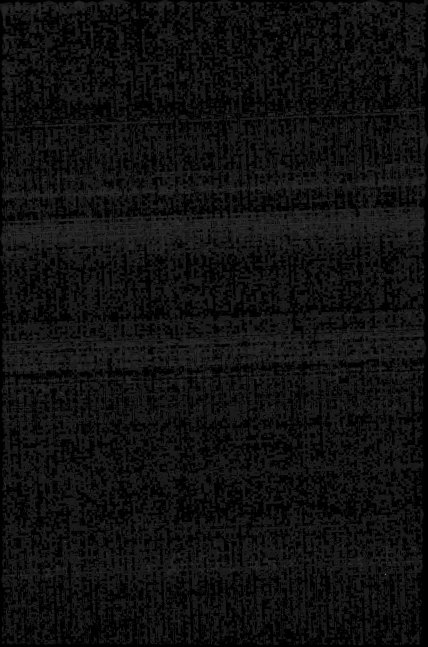

THE SPARTANS

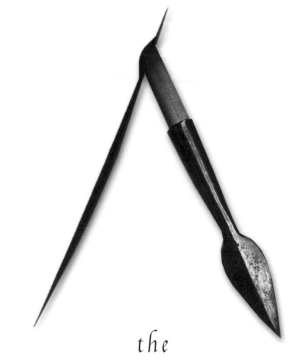

the

S P A R T A N S

ANDREW J. BAYLISS

OXFORD
UNIVERSITY PRESS

OXFORD

UNIVERSITY PRESS

Great Clarendon Street, Oxford, OX2 6DP,
United Kingdom

Oxford University Press is a department of the University of Oxford.
It furthers the University's objective of excellence in research, scholarship,
and education by publishing worldwide. Oxford is a registered trade mark of
Oxford University Press in the UK and in certain other countries

Published in the United States of America by Oxford University Press
198 Madison Avenue, New York, NY 10016, United States of America

British Library Cataloguing in Publication Data

Data available

Library of Congress Control Number: 2019951260

ISBN 978-0-19-885308-4

Printed in Great Britain by
Bell & Bain Ltd., Glasgow

CONTENTS

Acknowledgements   vii
List of Illustrations   ix

1. Go Tell the Spartans   1
2. Sparta's Civic Structure   26
3. The Spartan Lifestyle   46
4. Raising a Spartan   73
5. Spartan Women   95
6. Helots   111
7. The Later Reception of Sparta   129

Timeline   147
References   153
Further Reading on the Spartans   161
Index   165

ACKNOWLEDGEMENTS

When any book is written there are various people who need to be thanked, and this one is no exception. First of all, I would like to thank Andrea Keegan for the opportunity to write this book, and Jenny Nugee for her assistance throughout the writing process. I would also like to thank the anonymous readers for their clear and helpful feedback on both the proposal and the draft manuscript.

Second, I would like to acknowledge the debt I owe to my research colleagues working on Sparta. It was a genuine pleasure to absorb myself in your monographs, book chapters, journal articles, conference papers, and public lectures, and to try to translate such a vast output of scholarship into just 35,000 words. I am particularly grateful to Anton Powell, Steve Hodkinson, Tom Figueira, Paul Christesen, Ellen Millender, and Nigel Kennell for the encouragement, support, and earnest feedback for various research projects, not least this short book.

I would also like to thank my colleagues at the University of Birmingham, past and present, for their encouragement and support. The decision to make the new starter, who was then finishing up a book on Athens, emulate Alcibiades and defect to Sparta has had interesting consequences! I am also grateful to all of my students (PG and UG) who have chosen to work with me on dissertations relating to Sparta, and all the undergraduates who have taken my 'Sparta' module in in its various incarnations since 2008. I hope that all those fast-paced lectures on such diverse topics as Spartan education, military organization, sexuality, religion, dining practices, women, and the helots were as informative to attend as I found them useful when it came to writing this book.

I am also very grateful to the staff at Library at the British School at Athens, where a significant portion of this book was written, and to baristas at various cafés in Oxford and Athens who supplied me with the much-need caffeine while the more difficult process of pruning excess words was carried out.

Finally, I would like to thank my wife Vicky for her unstinting support throughout the whole process. Without her encouragement this book would never have come to light.

LIST OF ILLUSTRATIONS

1 Map of Greece and the Aegean World.   xii
   From *The Oxford Illustrated History of Greece and the
   Hellenistic World* edited by Boardman, Griffin, and Murray (2001).
   By permission of Oxford University Press.

2 Bronze statuette of draped Spartan warrior,
   c.510–500 BCE, Wadsworth Museum, Hartford, CT.   9
   Greek, probably Sparta. Draped Warrior, c.510–500 BCE.
   Bronze, 5 15/16 × *c*.2 1/16 × *c*.1 1/4in.
   (15.1 × *c*.5.3 × *c*.3.2 cm). Wadsworth Atheneum Museum
   of Art, Hartford, CT. Gift of J. Pierpont Morgan, 1917.815.
   Photography credit: Allen Phillips/Wadsworth Atheneum.

3 Apulian calyx-krater by the 'Painter of the Berlin
   Dancing Girl', *c*.420 BCE, Wellesley College Museum,
   Wellesley MA.   11
   Davis Museum at Wellesley College, Wellesley, MA.

4 Bronze facing of a Spartan shield captured at Pylos
   in 425 BCE, Athens, Agora Museum.   12
   American School of Classical Studies at Athens:
   Agora Excavations.

5 Glazed brick frieze of Persian soldiers, Susa,
   sixth century BCE.   16
   Lanmas/Alamy Stock Photo.

List of Illustrations

6 Map of Ancient Sparta. 27
From *Greece: An Oxford Archaeological Guide* by Christopher
Mee and Antony Spawforth (2001). By permission of
Oxford University Press.

7 View of the Roman-period theatre from the Spartan
acropolis. 28
Heritage Image Partnership Ltd/Alamy Stock Photo.

8 The pseudo-'Leonidas' marble bust, early fifth
century BCE, Archaeological Museum, Sparta. 36
iStockphoto.com/nexusimage.

9 Archaic period lead figurines from the sanctuary of
Artemis Orthia. 49
Courtesy of Philip Sapirstein (CC BY-NC-ND 2.0).

10 Bronze figurine of reclining banqueter, *c*.530–500 BCE,
British Museum. 55
© The Trustees of the British Museum.

11 Black-figure Laconian wine cup by the 'Hunt Painter',
c.550–540 BCE, Antikensammlung, Staatliche Museen
zu Berlin. 58
Marcus Cyron/Wikimedia Commons (CC BY-SA 3.0).

12 Bronze figurine of Spartan girl running or dancing,
c.520–500 BCE, British Museum. 97
© The Trustees of the British Museum.

13 Poster from the film *300* (2006), Warner Bros. Pictures. 139
PictureLux/The Hollywood Archive/Alamy Stock Photo.

14 'Sparty', the Michigan State University mascot (2007). 145
Joel Dinda/Flickr (CC BY 2.0).

Figure 1 Map of Greece and the Aegean World.

1

Go Tell the Spartans

I first encountered the Spartans at secondary school in Australia. I vividly recall learning how just 300 Spartans stood against millions of Persian invaders at the Battle of Thermopylae in 480 BCE. I remember being astounded by the Spartans' courage, outraged that they were betrayed by a fellow Greek, and awestruck that they chose to sacrifice their lives for Greek freedom on that final day rather than surrender. The epigram that was written for them afterwards—'Stranger, go tell the Spartans, that here, obedient to their words we lie'—was almost etched into my idealistic teenaged-brain.

But back then I somehow missed much of the Spartans' darker side, such as their callous exposure of disabled babies, the brutality of their state-run education system, and their ruthless exploitation of their helot slaves. I certainly do not recall learning that two Spartans survived Thermopylae, and both were so reviled by their peers that shame drove one of them to suicide. There was more to the Spartans than epic tales of courage. Sparta was a unique, often brutal society, considered an enigma even in antiquity, and this book will include the best and the worst of it. My intention here is not to provide a narrative history of Sparta, but rather to show what the Spartans were really like at the height of their power (550–371 BCE). I will begin by revisiting the story of the 300 Spartans at Thermopylae, separating the myths from reality.

'Le Mirage Spartiate'

The task of describing what the Spartans who fought at Thermopylae were really like is problematic because we possess almost no contemporary Spartan sources to tell their side of the story. All we really have left from Sparta are a few hundred lines of verse by the seventh-century BCE poets Tyrtaeus and Alcman, snippets from the writings of the third-century BCE Alexandrian-based Spartan scholar Sosibius, whose work survives only in later quotations known as 'fragments', and inscriptions. We rely instead on a large body of non-Spartan works ranging from the fifth century BCE to the fourth CE, which typically present Sparta as a radically unique society, unchanged for centuries, if not millennia. Modern scholars have even coined the term 'Spartan mirage' (originally 'le mirage Spartiate'), to describe how these later sources distorted and even invented facts about the Spartans to suit their own literary purposes.

The very first Greek historian to mention the Spartans, Herodotus of Halicarnassus (c.484–425 BCE), provides an excellent example of the difficulties we encounter when attempting to see beyond the Spartan mirage. Herodotus began his history of the conflict between the Greeks and the Persians by stating that he wanted 'to preserve the fame of the important and remarkable achievements'. The term Herodotus uses for 'remarkable achievements'— *thaumasta*—means things that make you stare wide-eyed with wonder, and Herodotus delivers on that promise when describing the Spartans' displays of courage at Thermopylae. Herodotus presents the Spartans as so unique that some modern experts argue that he actually introduces them to his Greek-speaking audience as foreigners whose unusual practices need to be explained like those of the Persians, Medes, Babylonians, Egyptians, and Scythians, and the other 'barbarians' he describes in other parts of his work.

Whereas Herodotus seems largely interested in telling a good story, some of the authors who followed in his footsteps used the image of Spartan uniqueness to fit an agenda. The Athenian Xenophon (*c*.430–354 BCE), who wrote a *Spartan Constitution* and a narrative history covering the period when the Spartans held hegemony over the Greek world, frequently highlights Sparta's uniqueness to demonstrate what he perceives as the superiority of Spartan society over other Greek states. Conversely, the Athenian historian Thucydides (*c*.460–400 BCE), who fought against the Spartans in the Peloponnesian war, and the Athenian orator Isocrates (436–338 BCE), who wrote works such as the *Panegyricus* eulogizing his native Athens, tend to present the Spartans' uniqueness as proof of their inferiority to the Athenians. For philosophers like the Athenian Plato (*c*.428–347 BCE), and Aristotle of Stageira (384–322 BCE), Sparta is merely a lens through which to examine the ideal society. Plato, who was generally favourable to Sparta, tends

3

to focus on aspects of Sparta that conform to his ideal state; Aristotle largely focuses on aspects of Spartan society that suit his thesis that Sparta was fundamentally flawed. The result is that not one of these contemporary sources—not even Xenophon's *Spartan Constitution*—aimed to provide us with a systematic, let alone objective, account of how Spartan society functioned.

Our later sources, including the most prolific source, the Boeotian biographer Plutarch (*c.*46–120 CE), were writing long after the Romans had conquered the Greeks, and were therefore separated from the Spartans of Thermopylae by what one modern expert recently called a 'great temporal and cultural distance'. The Sparta that they knew is often likened to a 'theme park', with the Spartans' strange practices attracting foreign visitors from around the Mediterranean. So when Plutarch writes about how Spartan society functioned in his 'biography' of the mythical Spartan lawgiver Lycurgus, he might actually be telling us about the Roman-period city rather than the Sparta of the men who fought at Thermopylae. We therefore cannot simply splice together snippets from sources separated by the best part of a millennium. Academics today tend to advocate a more contextual approach, which starts with contemporary sources like Herodotus and Xenophon who experienced Sparta first hand, before resorting to later and potentially less reliable sources like Plutarch. But this does not mean that we can simply ignore all the later sources that focus on the 'otherness' of the Spartans. The very notion of the Spartan mirage tells us that there really was something different about the Spartans. As one modern expert recently argued, the Spartan mirage demands an adjustment of our perspective, rather than a 'blanket rejection' of later sources.

Thermopylae: The 'Hot Gates'

By the time Herodotus was recording their story some fifty years later, the achievements of the Spartans at Thermopylae in the summer of 480 BCE were already legendary. But when the Spartan king Leonidas led out his tiny army of 300 citizen-soldiers and perhaps 700 helot attendants to fight against the Persians, none of them could have possibly imagined that some 2,500 years later people around the globe would be writing books about them, naming sporting teams after them, or treating their actions as anything out of the ordinary. That summer they were merely doing their duty as citizens of Sparta, a small but powerful Greek city located in Laconia in the south-east Peloponnese (see Figure 1). Their task was to join up with around 4,000 of their fellow Greeks from the Peloponnese and central Greece, and lead them against a truly massive invasion force led by the Persian king Xerxes (Xšayârša).

The other Greeks had chosen the Spartans to lead them against the Persians because they were the best soldiers in Greece, and they headed the 'Peloponnesian League' alliance. The size of the Spartans' task in many ways explains the legend that developed afterwards. The Persian kingdom was so large that Herodotus describes it as stretching from sunrise to sunset, and popular legend had it that Xerxes' army was three million strong, and that the accompanying pack animals alone drained a large lake! Yet the Spartans were not daunted by their task. When warned that there were so many archers in Xerxes' army that their arrows would darken they sky, the Spartan Dieneces responded tersely, 'good, we'll fight in the shade'.

Leonidas' allied army was so comparatively tiny, partly because Xerxes' kingdom was much larger than Greece, but also because Xerxes' invasion coincided with the quadrennial Olympic Games, when all Greeks were expected to suspend hostilities, and the annual pan-Dorian religious festival, the Carneia, when the Spartans and most of the Peloponnesians maintained a strict month-long truce. Modern scholars often speculate that Leonidas and his men were a token force tasked merely with holding Xerxes back until reinforcements could arrive after the Carneia, during which the Spartans reportedly eschewed all fighting, but imitated 'military discipline' by living in tents like warriors on campaign. It is also possible that Leonidas was leading a suicide squad. All the Spartans, including Leonidas, had living sons, and Plutarch says that before departing Leonidas instructed his wife Gorgo to marry a good man and bear strong children, which suggests that he had no intention of returning home. Diodorus (writing 60–30 BCE) provides an even more dramatic version; when the Spartan magistrates called ephors insisted Leonidas take more men to Thermopylae he refused, insisting their task was 'to die for the freedom of all'.

The odds were so stacked against the Spartans that Xerxes assumed they would run away. Herodotus reports that when the Spartans did not flee, Xerxes sent spies to see what they were doing. The Persian king was stunned to learn that some Spartans were wrestling naked and others were sitting around combing their long hair. Xerxes summoned Demaratus, an exiled Spartan king who was part of his entourage, and demanded to know what this behaviour meant. Demaratus warned him that Spartans always dressed their hair when they were about to risk their lives in battle. But Xerxes laughed off Demaratus' explanation, simply unable to believe that so few Spartans would dare to fight his immense army.

Herodotus says that after four days of waiting Xerxes became angry at what he perceived as Spartan 'folly and shamelessness', and ordered his men to attack. Later tradition had it that when Xerxes lost his temper he demanded that the Spartans surrender their arms to him, to which Leonidas retorted *môlon labe*, which means 'You come take them'. Sadly, the fact that Herodotus does not mention this suggests that it is a later embellishment; Herodotus had too much sense of drama to have omitted such a magnificent line.

The confidence the Spartans showed was not as foolhardy as Xerxes thought. Leonidas had chosen to defend the mountain pass at Thermopylae—literally the 'hot gates' because of the thermal springs at the pass—because it was a natural bottleneck on the main line of communication between northern and central Greece, where the numerical strength of the Persians could be negated. Alluvial deposits have caused the sea to recede by 5 km, but in Leonidas' day the Thermopylae pass was no more than 100 metres wide, and the sea came right up to the edge of the road. Leonidas chose to hold a particularly narrow stretch around 15–20 metres long where the pass was only 15.5 metres wide. Here, where the remains of the so-called 'Phocian wall' which

Leonidas' men rebuilt can be seen today, seemingly impenetrable cliffs rose steeply on the landward side, while the sea clashed against the rocks.

Leonidas could be confident that Xerxes would not use another route into Greece, as the road running through Thermopylae was the best for cavalry and wheeled carts, and being so close to the sea allowed Xerxes to maintain close contact with his enormous fleet of (allegedly) 1,207 warships and 3,000 transport vessels. What the Spartans did not know until they got to Thermopylae, was that there was another passage over the spine of the mountain which would allow the troops holding the narrowest point to be circumvented. Leonidas tasked the local Phocian troops with guarding this goat track. Modern commentators often criticize Leonidas' decision not to use his own men to defend this alternate route, or at least station a Spartan officer with them, but his choice made sense given that the Phocians knew the terrain. Regardless of the merits of his choice, Leonidas' decision to trust the Phocians to guard the backdoor would become a key part of the legendary story of Spartan bravery at Thermopylae.

The 300 Spartans

Leonidas and his men would have stood out from the other Greeks fighting at Thermopylae. Spartan citizens called themselves the *homoioi* ('equals' or 'similars'), and to reflect that equality their appearance was uniform (Figure 2). All Spartan citizens wore their hair long reputedly to make handsome men more handsome and ugly men more

Figure 2 Bronze statuette of draped Spartan warrior, *c.*510–500
BCE, Wadsworth Museum, Hartford, CT.

frightening. Spartan soldiers all wore red cloaks and tunics—the so-called *phoinikis*, or 'red outfit'—partly because red was considered the 'manliest' colour, and partly because it would help conceal bloodstains. Spartans also carried a wooden staff (*baktêrion*), which is sometimes compared to a modern army officer's 'swagger stick'. The Spartans' use of uniforms was unusual at the time, and seems designed to focus the enemy's attention on their intimidating conformity and unity.

The Spartans were also projecting an image of gentlemanly status. The Spartans' famous long hair would have required considerable maintenance, and was thought appropriate only for the leisured classes. As Aristotle put it, 'one who has long hair cannot easily perform any manual labour'. The Spartans' scarlet clothing was also a sign of wealth, because producing the red dye for each cloak, like the Tyrian purple later worn by Roman emperors, required harvesting thousands of murex shellfish; helpfully the *murex brandaris* teemed in Spartan coastal waters, allowing the Spartans to produce a colour-fast red dye the Roman writer Pliny the Elder (23–79 CE) later described as 'the best in Europe'. Nonetheless, Spartan cloaks are often described as *phaulos* (literally, 'slight' or 'insufficient'), which suggests that they were thin and shabby, although this is sometimes translated as 'short'.

Spartan infantrymen (like other Greeks) were known as 'hoplites'. They wore around 30 kg of bronze armour known as *ta hopla* ('the arms'), from which the term 'hoplite' is derived. On their heads they wore a helmet with a horsehair crest, with full face protection, the so-called

Figure 3 Apulian calyx-krater by the 'Painter of the Berlin Dancing Girl', *c.*420 BCE, Wellesley College Museum, Wellesley MA.

'Corinthian' helmet (see Figure 2). Modern experts suggest that the Corinthian helmet creates a state of psychological alertness owing to the lack of sensory stimulation, and made the wearer seem 'inhuman' because his face could not be seen. A few decades after Thermopylae the Spartans appear to have sacrificed protection for vision and hearing, replacing the Corinthian style of helmet with the conical *pilos* helmet (Figure 3). Leonidas and his men would each have worn a bronze breastplate, bronze leg-protectors, and carried a large (*c.*90cm circumference), bowl-like bronze-faced wooden shield (*aspis*) on their left arm (Figure 4). The Spartans reportedly emblazoned the Greek letter *lambda* on their shields, but the earliest evidence for this practice comes from an Athenian playwright who was writing several

11

Figure 4 Bronze facing of a Spartan shield captured at Pylos in 425 BCE, Athens, Agora Museum.

decades *after* Thermopylae. Leonidas and his men may have had personal emblems on their shields instead. Plutarch reports that a Spartan who was mocked for having a life-size image of a fly on his shield retorted, 'I come so close to the enemy that my emblem is seen by them in its true size'. Greek hoplites fought in ranks, with their shields protecting not just themselves, but also the right sides of their comrades. This 'phalanx' formation would have created a sense of solidarity and mutual dependence.

As weapons Spartans carried iron-headed spears made of ash (with bronze spikes on the butt end) in their right hands, and short stabbing swords (the *xiphos*) as a backup for when their spear shafts broke. Spartan swords were notoriously short, so short that the fourth-century BCE Athenian politician Demades joked that conjurors could swallow them whole; the blunt Spartan response was, 'Nonetheless, the Spartans reach the enemy with them'. The seventh-century BCE Spartan poet Tyrtaeus projects a similar image of the typical brave Spartan warrior in the lines 'Come on! Youths of Sparta, abounding in good men, thrust the shield in your left hand, brandishing your spear boldly not sparing your lives, for that is not the Spartan custom'.

The Spartans stood out from their fellow Greeks for their professionalism. Elsewhere in Greece only the wealthier citizens who could afford their own bronze armour fought as hoplites. At Athens, for example, the poorer citizens rowed on warships, or fought as light-armed troops. But Spartan citizens in Leonidas' day *all* fought as hoplites. According to Thucydides, the Spartans uniquely advanced into battle slowly accompanied by flute-players to ensure they 'keep in step and move forward steadily without breaking ranks'. At the time of Xerxes' invasion the Spartan army fought in five units called *lochoi*, with each *lochos* commanded by an officer known as a *lochagos* ('leader of a *lochos*'), and each *lochos* divided into smaller units known as 'sworn bands' (*enômotiai*), led by an officer called an *enômotarchês* ('ruler of the sworn band'). Later the Spartans changed this to six units known as *morai*, which comprised 'fiftieths' and sworn bands. Xenophon describes how orders were passed down from the Spartan king to senior officers called *polemarchoi*, and then to the *lochagoi*, and finally to the *enômotarchai*, who told their rankers what to do. The professionalism of this command structure was unparalleled at the time, and because of its similarity to modern military practice many modern translations render the Spartan officers as colonels, majors, and captains. The names that have been preserved for the five *lochoi* of Leonidas' day convey the Spartan wartime mindset: 'Devourer', 'Ravager', 'Rager', 'Thunder-cloud', and 'Leader of the Centre'. The Spartans who fought at Thermopylae lived up to these names.

Spartans were expected to fight to the death. Demaratus warned Xerxes that 'fighting together Spartans are the best men of all', because they have the law as their 'despot', and the law demands that they 'not flee from the fight before any multitudes of men, but stand firm in their ranks and either conquer or die'. Diodorus claims that Leonidas refused to take the whole Spartan army with him because it would have destroyed Sparta, 'for not one among them would dare to flee to reach safety'. This do-or-die attitude was even enshrined in the Spartan oath of citizenship—hence the 'sworn bands'—which bound them 'to not leave the ranks', that is, to prevail in battle or die trying.

This practice may date back to the so-called 'Battle of the Champions' (c.545 BCE), a duel between 300 picked men from Sparta and Argos designed to settle a territorial dispute, but effectively to determine which of the cities controlled the Peloponnese. At the end of the fighting three men remained standing—two Argives named Alcenor and Chromius who ran home to Argos believing that they had won the battle, and a Spartan named Othryadas who remained on the battlefield to strip the Argive corpses of their armour and build a victory monument. Later (unreliable) tradition had it that Othryadas wrote the dedication 'To Zeus, Guardian of Trophies' in his own blood. With both sides disputing the result, a full-scale pitched battle ensued. Casualties were heavy on both sides, but the Spartans emerged victorious, securing control of the territory and proving themselves masters of the Peloponnese. Herodotus says that after their victory the Spartans began to wear their hair long, and the Argives cropped theirs short in mourning, vowing not to grow their hair long until they reclaimed the territory. Yet after the Spartans' great victory, Othryadas committed suicide out of 'shame' that he alone of the 300 had survived.

Over the centuries that followed many, many Spartans—often commanding officers—ensured that they died in battle rather than suffer the sting of shame that Othryadas felt at surviving when his comrades did not. This became so much the norm that Thucydides reported, 'It was thought neither force nor famine could make the Spartans surrender their arms, but they would keep them and fight on as long as they were able to death'.

Few against Many

A Greek epigram set up after the battle proudly proclaimed, 'Here four thousand from the Peloponnese once fought three million'. Yet modern estimates of Xerxes' forces are in the region of 100,000 to 300,000 men. The Persians and Medes who made up the bulk of Xerxes' vast polyglot army wore loose caps called tiaras, embroidered sleeved tunics, scaled armour, and baggy trousers (Figure 5), an item of clothing that the ancient Greeks considered almost an abomination. As far as the Greeks—especially the Spartans—were concerned, proper men were not afraid to show off their body. Thucydides even claims that the Spartans 'invented' the Greek practice of exercising stark naked. The Persians' primary weapon was the bow—hence the jibe

Figure 5 Glazed brick frieze of Persian soldiers, Susa, sixth century BCE.

that their arrows would darken the sky. Xerxes' men also fought with spears, but crucially they were shorter than those wielded by the Spartans.

Despite the overwhelming odds against them, Leonidas and his men repelled Xerxes' massive force for two whole days. The Spartans and their fellow Greeks fought off wave after wave of Xerxes' men, starting with the Medes and Cissians, and—once he had grown very impatient—his crack troops, the so-called Immortals. These were 10,000 picked men who were called 'immortal' because they were immediately replaced when they fell. Diodorus claims the

Spartans killed so many of Xerxes' men that 'the entire area about the passes was strewn with dead bodies'. As Herodotus puts it, the Spartans 'made it clear to everyone, especially the king himself, that among so many people (*anthropoi*) he had few men (*andres*)'.

Herodotus says the Spartans fought with such skill that their efforts were 'worthy of mention'. He describes one repeated manoeuvre whereby the Spartans would turn their backs on the Persians feigning flight, but when the Persians rushed forward in pursuit, the Spartans would re-form their ranks and cut down their disorderly pursuers in large numbers. Diodorus borrows a line from Herodotus, describing the fighting as 'amazing', and revels in the bravery of the Spartans, asking 'who could be distinguished more than those men who were not equal even to the thousandth part of the enemy, yet dared to pit their manly excellence against the unbelievable multitudes?'.

Our sources give the impression that the fighting at Thermopylae was constant and relentless. Diodorus stresses that although the allied Greek forces began by fighting in relays, the Spartans soon refused to rest, with the older and younger soldiers vying to outdo each other in displaying their courage and prowess. But some academics have begun to question how realistic this might be, given that modern contact sports like ice hockey, rugby, and soccer, which run for only 60, 80, or 90 minutes respectively, tend to leave players physically exhausted. Nonetheless, while I am inclined to accept that there must have been breaks that our sources do not mention—for example, the Persians

must have halted while they worked out what to do next—
we have to remember that warfare is not sport. The adren-
alin rush from fighting for your very life means that soldiers
in the heat of battle are often capable of feats of endurance
that modern athletes are not. It is easier to break through the
metaphorical 'wall' when your life depends upon it.

Enter the 'Nightmare'—Ephialtes

We will never know whether Leonidas really hoped to hold
Thermopylae. For at the end of the second day the Greeks
were betrayed by one of their own, a local Trachinian named
Ephialtes, who told Xerxes about the goat track over the
mountain. The fact that Ephialtes' name means 'nightmare'
in both ancient and modern Greek (from the verb *epiallo-
mai*, 'I jump on', deriving from the common nightmare of
an incubus/succubus leaping onto the sleeper's chest) is
mere coincidence, but it certainly adds to the legendary
nature of the story. The Spartans later put a price on
Ephialtes' head, and although he was murdered for an
entirely unrelated reason, the Spartans rewarded his killer
anyway.

Xerxes acted swiftly, ordering Ephialtes to lead his general
Hydarnes and the Immortals along the goat path. Herodotus
says that they set off 'at lamp-lighting time' and reached the
summit by dawn. But trekking through the mountains in
the dark seems a rather risky option, so there might be some
exaggeration here. When the Phocians who were guarding
the path were alerted to the approach of the Persians by the

sound of their footsteps they made a critical error, withdrawing to higher ground in the mistaken assumption that they were the Persians' primary target. Rather unsurprisingly, Hydarnes was terrified that the Phocians were actually Spartans. But when Ephialtes assured him they were not—sometimes thought to be a sign that Spartans already had the letter *lambda* emblazoned on their shields—the Persians swept through the open doorway leaving the Phocians in their wake.

Leonidas learned that he was about to be surrounded before it was too late for his whole army. Some said deserters warned him, others that Leonidas' seer, Megistias, foretold that death was coming at dawn after examining the sacrificial victims, which sounds a little too convenient. Whatever the case Leonidas dismissed the majority of his forces, but opted to remain at his post to buy enough time for the rest to withdraw safely. Herodotus believed that Leonidas chose to remain behind both to achieve 'glory', and to fulfil an oracle from Delphi which foretold that Sparta would be destroyed by the Persians unless a Spartan king was killed. Some modern scholars think that this oracle was a *post eventum* invention designed to explain away a humiliating defeat for the Spartans. But it has also been suggested that Leonidas personally engineered the oracle to suit his purpose on that final day. It might even be that the Spartans were mindful of the fact that they were fighting in contravention of the normal rules of the Carneia festival, and essentially offered themselves as a kind of human sacrifice to avoid Sparta incurring divine displeasure.

'Tonight We Dine in Hades'

On the final morning Leonidas and his remaining Spartans took the fight to the Persians. They were accompanied by the hoplites from Thespiae, who refused to leave with the other allies. The hoplites from Thebes remained on the final day too, but rather controversially, Leonidas is said to have detained them as hostages to ensure that Thebes did not go over to the Persians. Advancing into a wider, and therefore less safe part of the pass, the Spartans fought with such gusto that Herodotus describes them as 'frenzied'. Diodorus reports that because the Spartans were ready to die, they 'performed heroic and incredible deeds'. Some modern scholars think the Spartans were attempting to achieve a 'beautiful death' (*kalos thanatos*), a concept based on Tyrtaeus' poetry which told generation after generation of Spartans—Plato (*c.*428–347 BCE) described Sparta as 'replete' with Tyrtaeus' songs—that 'it is a beautiful thing for a good man to die having fallen in the front ranks fighting for his fatherland'.

By the time Hydarnes and the Immortals appeared behind them, Leonidas and many of his men had achieved a beautiful death. They took many brave Persians with them, including two of Xerxes' half-brothers. Herodotus says that many Persians were trampled underfoot, and others were pushed into the sea, by the frenzied 'shove' (*othismos*) of the Spartan phalanx. In scenes reminiscent—surely intentional—of Homer's epic poem the *Iliad*, in which the Greeks led by the *Spartan* king Menelaus fought the Trojans for possession of the hero Patroclus' body, hurling the

Trojans back three times, Herodotus says Leonidas' men by 'much shoving' and 'manly virtue' threw back the Persians *four* times.

Their fate sealed by the arrival of the Immortals, the remaining Spartans and Thespians withdrew to a small bluff to make their final stand. In so doing, they lost touch with the Thebans who surrendered. Xerxes later had these men branded on their foreheads as a token of slavery. By now most of the Spartans had broken their spears and were fighting only with swords or knives. Some fought on with just their bare hands and teeth as they faced the Persians who bore down on them on all sides. But even then the Spartans proved such formidable opponents that many Persians preferred to shoot them down with the arrows rather than fight them hand-to-hand. In the end the Persians probably really did darken the sky with their arrows!

Few modern commentators trust Diodorus' rather bizarre story of Leonidas launching a last-ditch night attack on Xerxes' pavilion, with the Persians panicking and Xerxes escaping only by cowardly flight into the night. In a (probably) facetious work entitled *On the Malice of Herodotus*, Plutarch even criticized Herodotus for having obscured Leonidas' bravest act by omitting the night raid, and promised to redress this and other omissions in a biography of Leonidas, although no such work has survived. We can also discount Diodorus' claim that when Leonidas' men begged him to lead them against the Persians he ordered them to prepare their breakfast quickly because they would soon be dining in Hades (i.e. hell). Like *môlon labe*, this one-liner was a later embellishment not known by Herodotus.

21

After the battle Xerxes was so angry that he cut off Leonidas' head and set it up on a pike. The Persian losses were so humiliatingly high—Herodotus provides a suspiciously round figure of 20,000—that Xerxes was forced to engage in an elaborate charade, leaving all the Spartans unburied for everyone to see, but hiding hordes of his own dead so that no one would see just how many Persians had been killed by so few Spartans. Herodotus gleefully reports that Greek visitors to the site were not fooled, and they were able to discern that many of the corpses of 'Spartans' that Xerxes pointed out for visitors to see were in fact their helot attendants.

Victory in Defeat?

At first glance Thermopylae seems a disastrous defeat. But Diodorus argues that the Spartans' bravery in the face of such overwhelming odds proved inspirational to their fellow Greeks in subsequent battles against the Persians, namely the Athenian-led victory over Xerxes' massive armada at the Battle of Salamis later that summer, which prompted Xerxes to return home, and the Battle of Plataea the following summer, when the Spartans led nearly 40,000 Greek hoplites to victory over an army of supposedly 300,000 Persians commanded by Xerxes' nephew Mardonius. Diodorus stresses that in these later battles which put paid to Persian ambitions of conquering Greece, 'when the deeds of these men were remembered, the Persians were panic-stricken, whereas the Greeks were driven to similar courageous exploits', and even claims that the Spartans 'were more responsible for the common freedom of the Greeks' than those who fought at Salamis and Plataea.

After the repulse of the Persians a memorial with a stone lion was set up on that small bluff where the Spartans made their final stand. On it was written that famous epigram by Simonides of Ceos (c.556–468 BCE), 'Stranger, go tell the Spartans, that here, obedient to their words we lie'. A monument that listed all the names and patronymics of the Spartiates who fought at Thermopylae was set up at Sparta. The Roman-period travel writer Pausanias (c.110–180 CE) describes the monument, and Herodotus clearly saw it because he says he learned all of the names of these 'men worthy of record' when he travelled to Sparta. Pausanias also reports that the Spartans built the so-called 'Persian Stoa' in their marketplace (*agora*) from the spoils of the war against Xerxes. Forty years after the battle Leonidas' descendant King Pausanias brought his remains back to Sparta; a shrine—the Leonidaeum—was built in the Hellenistic period, and games were held in Leonidas' honour. Only Spartan citizens could compete at these games, which suggests the Spartans chose to ignore the contributions of the other Greeks at Thermopylae, most unfairly given the Thespians shared their fate on that last day.

Aristodemus the Coward?

But the story of the Spartans at Thermopylae does not end there. The Spartan veneration of those who died at Thermopylae stands in stark contrast to the fate of two Spartans who survived the fighting: Pantites and Aristodemus.

Pantites had been sent away as a messenger, but when he returned to Sparta he was 'dishonoured' and hanged himself out of shame. Aristodemus' story was more complicated. He and another Spartan named Eurytus were afflicted with an eye problem (*ophthalmia*) which impaired their vision so badly that Eurytus had to be led by hand to the fighting on the last day by his helot attendant. Exactly what afflicted Eurytus and Aristodemus is unclear, but experts have argued that they might have been temporarily struck blind by the psychological trauma of two days of relentless fighting. The sightless Eurytus plunged into the melee and died. But Aristodemus chose not to join him. So when he returned home he was reviled as a 'trembler' (*tresas*); Herodotus reports no Spartan would share fire with him or even speak to him.

Aristodemus attempted to make up for his disgrace the following summer at the Battle of Plataea, rushing out from the Spartan ranks in a frenzy, and 'achieving great deeds', before falling. Herodotus felt that Aristodemus was by far the bravest of all the Greek fighters at Plataea, and was mystified by the fact that the Spartans refused to accept that Aristodemus was brave on the grounds that he had wanted to die. Herodotus could only explain their attitude as jealousy, and many academics have condemned the Spartans' treatment of Aristodemus as unfair. It has even been suggested that Aristodemus and Pantites met more sinister ends, with both being silenced to ensure that nothing that contradicted the official Sparta version of events at Thermopylae leaked out. But I prefer to interpret this story as showing that as far as Spartans were concerned being brave meant sacrificing your life not because you wanted to die, but in spite of wanting to live. Like Eurytus, Aristodemus could have been brave enough to perish with his comrades, which is why the Spartans remembered him as a coward, rather than a brave man. It was harsh, but Sparta was a harsh place.

2
Sparta's Civic Structure

Although the Spartans called themselves 'equals', Sparta was actually a rigidly hierarchical society, comprising: (1) the citizens (*homoioi*) who lived in the town of Sparta itself; (2) an intermediate class of subordinate peoples called *perioikoi*, who lived in the surrounding territory, hence their name which means 'the dwellers around'; (3) their servile labourers called 'helots'. So when we talk about 'Spartans' we might mean the *homoioi*, but we could also mean the *perioikoi*, the helots, or even a number of other lesser-known Spartan social classes who crop up in our sources.

Even more confusingly for the modern reader, the people we know as 'Spartans' were not really called Spartans. We call them Spartans because they came from the city of Sparta, which might derive from the Greek verb *speirô* ('I sow'), making Sparta 'the sown land' (Figures 6 and 7). The Spartans called themselves Spartiates, but outsiders usually called them 'Lacedaemonians'. This name dates back to Bronze Age Linear B tablets which mention 'the Lacedaemonian' (*ra-ke-da-mi-ni-jo*), and reflects the fact that Sparta was not just a city, but what the Greeks called a *polis* (often translated 'city-state'),

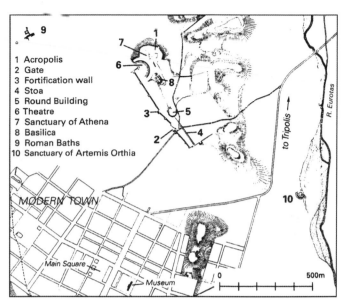

Figure 6 Map of Ancient Sparta.

comprising the city of Sparta—five villages (each called an *obê*), with four (Pitana, Limnae, Mesoa, Cynosoura) clustered around a small acropolis (literally 'high-city') near the bank of the Eurotas river, and the fifth (Amyclae) located around five kilometres to the south—and the surrounding 8,500 km² of countryside. If that was not confusing enough, the Spartans also called the whole territory they controlled neither Sparta nor Lacedaemon, but 'Lakônikê gê' ('Laconian land'). So Spartans often appear in our sources not as Spartans, or Lacedaemonians, but as 'Laconians'.

Figure 7 View of the Roman-period theatre from the Spartan acropolis.

Spartan Citizens—the So-called *'Homoioi'*

Spartan citizens were known as either *homoioi* or Spartiates (*Spartiatai* in Greek). This status was accorded only to sons of Spartiates who had been trained in the brutal Spartan upbringing, and to maintain their citizenship all Spartiates up to the age of 60 had to serve in the army. Spartiates were also required to dine together each night in communal mess groups, providing monthly contributions of barley, wine, olive oil, cheese, and pork from the produce of their estates.

Our later sources claim that an ancient Spartan lawgiver, Lycurgus, divided up Spartan territory so that each of the then 9,000 Spartan citizens received an equal plot of land (*klaros*) that was inalienable, thus ensuring that all the Spartan citizens were equals in terms of wealth. Plutarch (*c*.46–120 CE) claims that when Lycurgus returned from abroad at harvest time he saw equal heaps of grain piled up side by side, and remarked to the bystanders that 'the whole of Lakônikê seems like many brothers recently divided it'. Lycurgus' system was said to have functioned effectively for centuries until a selfish ephor, Epitadeus, wanted to punish his son and changed the law so that he could sell his plot to someone else, thus depriving his son of his *klaros* and his Spartiate status.

But today the story that each Spartiate was allotted an equal *klaros* of land at birth is doubted by many academics, and few would argue that Lycurgus, who was traditionally said to have lived either in the 900s or 700s BCE, ever existed. Critics also point out that the *klaros* system would have been fiendishly difficult to administer; after all not every citizen would have just one son to inherit his plot. Furthermore, Aristotle (384–322 BCE) reveals that in the seventh-century BCE poor Spartans actively clamoured for a redistribution of land generations, if not centuries, after Lycurgus had supposedly already redistributed it! It seems far more likely that it was not 'Lycurgus', but rather the conquest of Messenia in the seventh century BC that made Spartan 'equality' possible. Events are shrouded in myth, but sometime around the late 700s BCE the Spartiates marched round the Taygetus mountain range and seized the fertile Pamisus valley in Messenia. After a long and bloody war of resistance by the locals the Spartiates took full control of Messenia around 650 BCE. The Messenian lands were distributed among the Spartiates as spoils of war, and those Messenians who did not flee in defeat were enslaved to work the land as 'helots'.

This is why the Spartiates who served at Thermopylae with Leonidas stood apart from their fellow Greeks: exploiting helot labour freed Spartiates from the need to work, and allowed them to spend their days training their bodies, producing what was effectively a standing army of professional citizen soldiers. Xenophon (*c.*430–354 BCE) says that the only work that was permitted for Spartiates was that which promoted 'freedom for the *polis*', and some of the later sources state outright that Spartiates were debarred from manual labour altogether. However, it was probably more the case that when the Spartans set the rules of citizenship (probably in the sixth century BCE) they fixed the property qualification sufficiently high that no citizen should ever need to work for a living, thereby excluding those who made their money from trade alone.

Calling themselves the *homoioi* and dressing like high-status gentlemen allowed the Spartans to conceal the fact that there was significant disparity of wealth among the so-called 'equals'. Their uniform appearance was part of a compromise between richer and poorer Spartiates. Thucydides (*c.*460–400 BCE) claims that 'the Spartans were the first to adopt a more modest style of dress... and there the rich adopted a lifestyle more on equal footing with the poor'. Later sources tell us that coloured dyes were banned for non-military clothing on the grounds that it was vanity, and that no Spartan citizen was allowed to go outside better dressed than another. But by focusing on the rich having to adopt more modest dress within the confines of Spartan society, our sources are missing the fact that poorer Spartans were required to 'style up' with their elaborately braided hair and expensively-dyed (albeit shabby) military cloaks, and that outside Sparta the *homoioi* were presenting a collective image of modestly dishevelled rich men, rather like a cash-poor country squire today wearing a battered—but once high-quality—tweed jacket.

However, all this only masked the problem of inequality in Sparta, which has been likened to a 'spreading cancer' because it ultimately destroyed Sparta from within. There were probably never more than 10,000 Spartiates, and over the course of the fifth and fourth centuries BCE their numbers declined steeply as many citizens found themselves no longer able to make the substantial food contributions required to retain their place in a common mess. By 371 BCE, when the Thebans effectively ended Spartan greatness by defeating them in the Battle of Leuctra, there were little more than 1,000 *homoioi*. No wonder then that Aristotle said that Sparta was destroyed by 'scantiness of men' (*oliganthrôpia*).

'Inferiors'

The impact of inequality at Sparta can be seen in the rise of a subclass of Spartans called 'inferiors' (*hypomeiones*). We know the name of just one inferior, a certain Cinadon, who was so disgruntled at his inferior status that he plotted to overthrow the Spartan state in 399 BCE. After he was arrested and asked what he hoped to achieve by his plot, his blunt reply was, 'To be inferior to no one in Sparta'.

Xenophon describes Cinadon as 'young in body and stout in spirit', which means that he cannot have been deemed inferior in terms of his physical or mental qualities. This has led modern scholars to assume that men like Cinadon were inferior owing to poverty, and had been deprived of full citizen status because they were unable to make the necessary mess contributions.

There is probably a connection between the inferiors and another Spartan subclass, the so-called *mothakes*. These participated in the public upbringing alongside the sons of Spartiates as 'brothers by adoption' (*syntrophoi*). Until quite recently most academics thought that the *mothakes* were illegitimate sons of Spartiates by helot women, lumping them together with another subgroup of Spartans called *nothoi* (literally 'bastards'). But there is a growing consensus that the *mothakes* were actually the sons of inferiors whose participation in the upbringing was sponsored by wealthy Spartans. This interpretation sees the Spartans setting up a 'safety-net' to allow the sons of the disfranchised to regain their place amongst the *homoioi* via private patronage. Three prominent fifth-century BCE Spartan generals—Lysander, Gylippus, and Callicratidas—were all said to have started life as *mothakes*.

'Tremblers'

Our sources also mention 'tremblers' (*tresantes*), Spartiates who had shown cowardice in battle. Tremblers were reportedly treated with contempt by other Spartiates. They were compelled to shave off half their beard and to wear patchwork cloaks, presumably both in order to make them look ridiculous and to mark them out. Xenophon says that no Spartiate would choose a trembler as a son-in-law or father-in-law, and that every Spartiate would be 'ashamed' to even have a trembler in his mess or as a wrestling partner. Tremblers were picked last in ball games, banished to 'insulting' positions in choruses, and forced to yield to younger men—a striking inversion of Spartan norms whereby younger men always gave way to their elders. Xenophon declares rather darkly, 'when this sort of disgrace is imposed on cowards I wonder not that death seems preferable to such a life of dishonour and shame', and we have already seen that Aristodemus, who is in fact the only attested Spartiate to suffer the dreaded label 'trembler', seized the first opportunity to end his own life in a blaze of glory by charging out from the ranks at the Battle of Plataea.

But some modern scholars have started questioning whether Spartan cowards really were punished in this way. After all, Herodotus says nothing about Aristodemus having to shave off half his beard or wear a patchwork cloak, and other Spartans accused of cowardice in battle were formally exiled or condemned to death. Some cowards escaped punishment altogether. When 120 Spartiates surrendered to the Athenians at Sphacteria in 425 BCE the Spartans briefly imposed 'dishonour' (*atimia*) on them, but quickly revoked it because many were prominent citizens. Later, when several hundred Spartans panicked and fled the battlefield at Leuctra in 371 BCE, the Spartan king Agesilaus infamously refused to degrade them, stating that 'it is right that our current laws be valid—from tomorrow'. But it would be dangerous to read too much into these seemingly aberrant cases, which could well be the exceptions that prove the rule for Spartan cowards.

The *Perioikoi*

At some point before the eighth century BCE the Spartans gained the allegiance/submission of various communities living around them in Lakônikê, who became known as the *perioikoi*. Although the *perioikoi* were ethnically and linguistically indistinguishable from the Spartiates, and shared the designation 'Lacedaemonians' with them, they were subordinate to them. The *perioikoi* were free to trade with the outside world, but they had no control over foreign policy, and were required to follow the *homoioi* into war without any say in the matter. For this reason some academics categorize the *perioikoi* as 'second-class citizens' of Sparta.

The relationship between the Spartiates and the *perioikoi* was somewhat unusual. Regions even a fraction of the size of Lakônikê were typically made up of dozens of *poleis*, which were either fiercely independent or formally bound together in a federal league. But the *perioikoi* were neither citizens of fully independent *poleis* nor equals in a league with the Spartans. Rather, they appear to have been free citizens of subordinate *poleis* within the Spartan state. This helps explain why Isocrates (436–338 BCE) claimed that the Spartans enslaved the souls of the *perioikoi* as thoroughly as they enslaved the bodies of the helots.

We do not know how many *perioikoi* there were, how many communities of *perioikoi* there were, and we cannot even be certain whether they lived in communities known as *poleis, komai* ('villages'), or both. Later legend had it that when Lycurgus distributed *klaroi* to just 9,000 Spartiates he also arranged 30,000 *klaroi* for the *perioikoi*, which suggests that the *perioikoi* outnumbered the Spartiates significantly. Modern scholars typically suggest that the estates of the *perioikoi* comprised around 30 per cent of the arable land in Lakônikê. The small landholdings of the *perioikoi* compared to the Spartiates reflects not numerical inferiority, but inferiority of wealth. Whereas all Spartiates were landed gentry, only some of the *perioikoi* would have been wealthy landowners. Many of the *perioikoi* would have been engaged in the economic activities denied to the Spartiates: manufacturing, overseas trade (all the main harbours in Lakônikê were perioikic), and the exploitation of mineral resources. The *perioikoi* were probably responsible for much of surviving 'Spartan' art, for example the famous fifth-century BCE marble bust erroneously linked to Leonidas (Figure 8), and it seems likely that famous 'Lacedaemonian' artists, like Gitiadas who designed the ornate bronze decorations at the Spartan sanctuary of Athena Chalkioikos ('Bronze House'), were *perioikoi* rather than Spartiates. Consequently, some art historians suggest it would be better to refer to 'Laconian' rather than 'Spartan' art.

One recent survey argued that without the *perioikoi* Sparta would have been 'no more than an average power', because the wealthiest of the *perioikoi* boosted Sparta's armies by serving as hoplites in the phalanx alongside the *homoioi*. When warning Xerxes of what would face him after defeating just 300 Spartans at Thermopylae, the exiled Spartan

Figure 8 The pseudo-'Leonidas' marble bust, early fifth century BCE, Archaeological Museum, Sparta.

king Demaratus stressed that Xerxes would soon encounter not only thousands of Spartiates just like Leonidas and his 300, but also thousands more men who lived around them, who were *kaloi k'agathoi*—literally the 'fine and good', but effectively meaning 'gentlemen'—which must have meant the *perioikoi*. Demaratus was correct in his prophecy, because the following summer Leonidas' nephew Pausanias led 5,000 Spartiates and 5,000 *perioikoi*, with support from 30,000 allied Greek hoplites, to victory over the Persians at the Battle of Plataea.

As Spartiate numbers declined rapidly in the fifth century BCE the Spartans began to rely increasingly heavily on the military contributions of the *perioikoi*. By 418 BCE, at the Battle of Mantinea—according to Thucydides the biggest land battle in Greece since Plataea—the ratio between the *perioikoi* and the *homoioi* was probably around 60:40, and by the disastrous Spartan defeat at Leuctra in 371 BCE it was 70:30. Many modern experts think that as the Spartans became more reliant on the *perioikoi* they allowed them to fight alongside them in the same units. It seems likely then that the *perioikoi* also wore red in battle, or else the enemy would have easily seen the difference between them and the Spartiates. An exception might be the *skiritai*, who lived in villages to the north of Sparta itself, and whose role was to fight in their own unit as an advance guard. The strength of the Lacedaemonian identity can be seen in the fact that whereas the Spartans sent officials called 'foreigner-leaders' (*xenagoi*) to summon the allies who fought in their armies, they appear to have sent regular Spartan troops to muster the *perioikoi*.

Some academics believe that the *perioikoi* who served in the Spartan army must have undergone part of the harsh Spartan upbringing. We know that sometimes foreign boys participated in the upbringing, and that the Spartans called them *trophimoi* (foster brothers). Notable foreigners who reportedly received a Spartan education include Xenophon's sons Gryllus and Diodorus, and Phocus, the wastrel son of the notoriously ascetic fourth-century BCE Athenian general Phocion who, like the Spartans, shunned shoes even on campaign. It would make sense for the Spartans to have expected the *perioikoi* who fought with them to have shared in at least some of their rigorous upbringing as foster brothers; how else would they have trusted them to fight alongside them in their 'sworn bands'?

The Helots

The lowest rung of the Spartan ladder was occupied by the servile population of 'helots', whose labour made the Spartiates' gentleman-warrior lifestyle possible. The Spartiates were so heavily dependent upon helot labour that one modern scholar recently called them 'the alimentary canal' of Spartan society. But it might be more accurate to view the Spartans as 'parasitic', feeding off the labours of their helots who outnumbered their Spartiate masters by perhaps as much as 10:1. Mutual fear probably explains both why the Spartans treated the helots so harshly that Plutarch labelled their treatment 'callous and brutal', and why the helots hated their masters so much that Xenophon reports they 'would gladly eat them even raw'.

Whereas slaves in ancient Greece were typically heterogeneous foreign captives purchased from slave traders, the helots were said to be the descendants of the original Greek inhabitants of Laconia and Messenia who had been enslaved by the Spartans. This mythic tradition makes the

Spartans a curious mix of bad and good, 'Dorian' outsiders from central Greece who displaced the aboriginal 'Achaeans' from Laconia, but doing so in a good cause, to help the great-great-grandsons of the great hero Heracles (perhaps better known as Hercules) reclaim their lost ancestral homeland. Of the descendants of Heracles, Temenos became the king of Argos, Cresphontes received Messenia, and Leonidas' ancestor Aristomachus gained the throne of Sparta. This tradition had a long history, dating back at least to the surviving fragments of the seventh-century BCE poetry of Tyrtaeus, who talks of the Spartans leaving the Dorian heartland 'windy Erineus' with the descendants of Heracles for the Peloponnese.

But the Spartans become the villains of the piece when they turn on their fellow Dorian invaders in Messenia, seizing their farmlands and enslaving their defeated brethren. The Spartans were attracted by the fertility of Messenia, which Tyrtaeus calls 'good to plough, good to sow'. The conquest of Messenia was remembered as a long and bloody operation, with Tyrtaeus explicitly stating that the conquest took nineteen years to complete. Some decades later the Messenians staged a bloody rebellion in which they appear to have inflicted heavy defeats on the Spartans. But the Spartans eventually overcame the Messenian resistance, reputedly inspired by the warlike elegies Tyrtaeus composed to encourage them to fight bravely. The victorious Spartans exacted a heavy price, with Tyrtaeus describing the Messenians as labouring 'like asses exhausted under great loads, under powerful necessity to bring their masters half the fruit their ploughed land produced'.

Today we tend to see the story of a 'Dorian invasion' as a rationalizing myth, with Classicists and archaeologists more likely now to speak of a Dorian 'ethnogenesis' (literally the birth of an ethnic group), with the Spartans and most of the other Peloponnesians (including the Messenians) developing a homogenous regional material culture and identity over time. But that does not make the Spartans' brutal treatment of the helots any more palatable from our perspective.

Neodamodeis

Some helots were able to gain their freedom, usually in exchange for military service. These freedmen gained the title *neodamodeis* (literally 'new members of the *dêmos*'), which can be translated as 'newly enfranchised'. But that translation belies their true status, because these new men did not become Spartiates or even *perioikoi*, but rather free men who were still very much subject to the Spartans.

Thucydides is the first source to mention the *neodamodeis*, noting that around 420 BCE some other ex-helots who had fought under the Spartan general Brasidas—the so-called Brasideioi—were settled on Sparta's border with Elis alongside them. Unfortunately Thucydides does this without explanation, throwing the *neodamodeis* into his narrative as if we already know who these newly enfranchised men are. Modern scholars typically assume that Thucydides' testimony suggests that one of the duties of these freedmen living on the border would have been to capture runaway helots and ensure that they were returned to their estates, which may have made these freedmen look like collaborators in the eyes of their former fellow slaves.

Spartan Government

Most ancient Greek states were governed by democracy (e.g. Athens), oligarchy, literally 'rule by the few' (e.g. Corinth), or an autocrat, either a king (e.g. Macedon), or a 'tyrant' (e.g. Syracuse in Sicily). But Sparta had what ancient Greek commentators called a 'mixed' constitution, which blended kingship, oligarchy, and democracy. When Herodotus visited Sparta in the mid-fifth century BCE, the Spartans told him they had been the 'most lawless' (*kakonomôtatoi*) of all the Greeks until centuries earlier when Lycurgus laid the foundation for the entire Spartan way of life, including the state laws, the military institutions, and the communal dining practices. Lycurgus even allegedly travelled to the Oracle of Delphi to have this arrangement endorsed by the god Apollo. Today we call Lycurgus' constitutional brainchild the 'Great Rhetra', from *rhetra*, literally 'saying', and the Spartan word for 'decree'. According to Plutarch, the *rhetra* decreed the division of the Spartans into tribes and *obai*, the setting up a council of thirty Elders, the holding of regular citizen assemblies with 'the power belonging to the people'. By the time Thucydides was writing in the late fifth century BCE, Lycurgus' reforms were believed to have brought about centuries of harmony, and protected the Spartans from the civil strife that afflicted almost all every other mainland Greek *polis* in the sixth century BCE.

However, as noted earlier, Lycurgus was almost certainly mythical, since neither of our earliest surviving sources for Sparta—Tyrtaeus and Alcman—makes any mention of him. Nonetheless later generations of Spartans came to believe that Lycurgus had set up all the rules of Sparta, and they may even have fabricated the Great Rhetra to legitimize the story as the power of the Lycurgus myth grew. Most academics today believe that the Spartan constitution was the product of a more slow evolution, and that the 'austere' Spartan lifestyle which later generations attributed to Lycurgus only really came into being a few decades before Leonidas and his men stunned the world with their displays of courage at Thermopylae.

Unlike most other Greek states, Sparta had kings. But even more unusually, Sparta was not a monarchy, but a dyarchy, with two kings from two separate royal houses—the Agiads and Eurypontids. So anyone familiar with the Spartans only through the story of Thermopylae is unlikely to have encountered Leonidas' co-king, Leotychides, who led the Greeks to victory over Xerxes' forces at the Battle of Mycale in 479 BCE. The Spartans claimed that this peculiar arrangement dated back to the eleventh century BCE when their first king, Aristomachus, died before his wife gave birth to twin sons, Eurysthenes and Procles. The Spartans did not know which boy should be the rightful king because their mother refused to reveal which was the eldest, so they made them both kings. But as nice as this story sounds, we cannot really hope to know the truth of how this unique arrangement came about.

Unlike the story told in the film *300*, in which Leonidas unilaterally brings about war against the Persians by kicking

Xerxes' ambassador down a well, Spartan kings were not absolute monarchs. Their main role was as military commanders, although they were also priests of Zeus, and keepers of oracles from Delphi. Leonidas' half-brother Cleomenes took this latter role so seriously he stole scrolls recording oracles from the Athenian acropolis. Spartan kings could not declare war or even muster an army on their own; the elected magistrates the ephors (literally 'overseers') did that for them, and two ephors accompanied the kings on campaign to keep an eye on them. Spartan kings could be fined, exiled, and deposed, and were even obliged to swear a monthly oath that they would reign according to the laws of the state, with the ephors swearing in turn that as long as the kings kept their oath they would 'preserve the kingship unshaken'. This monthly exchange of oaths highlights how precarious the position of Spartan kings really was.

The Spartan constitution resembled an oligarchy in that Sparta had a small ruling council, the *gerousia* ('the Elders'). This council of thirty was made up of twenty-eight men aged over 60 who were elected for life, plus the two kings regardless of their age. So Leonidas, who was aged around 60 at the time of Thermopylae, was perhaps not yet an 'old man' when he became one of the Elders. The elections for this office were rather comical—Aristotle calls them 'childish'—a Spartiate was locked in a room with a writing tablet, and as the candidates were brought forward, he would write down the number of the one who received the loudest acclamation. Herodotus reports that if the kings were absent for a decision-making vote by the *gerousia*, their nearest kin

43

(i.e. other royal family members) serving on the council could cast a proxy vote on behalf of the absent king as well as their own. This has led some modern scholars to assume that the *gerousia* tended to be dominated by the wealthiest Spartan families.

Sparta can also be seen to resemble a democracy in that Sparta had a citizen assembly (*ekklêsia*) where Spartiates could vote on bills put forward by the *gerousia*, a process known as *probouleusis* ('previous deliberation'). But Spartan citizens in the assembly could not discuss or amend bills; the assembly's role was effectively to rubber-stamp decisions that had already been made by the *gerousia*. Plutarch says that this arrangement came about because the Spartan citizens had once played too active a role in the decision-making process, 'twisting' the resolutions put forward by the *gerousia*. Consequently a blunt amendment was inserted into Sparta's constitution: 'if the people choose crookedly the kings and elders shall set it aside'. As with voting for the *gerousia*, the Spartiates in the assembly made their decisions by shouting. This could prove difficult to assess with precision; when the Spartans were voting on whether to go to war against Athens in 432 BCE the ephor Sthenelaidas ordered the citizens to move into groups in favour of war and against so that they could be counted accurately. It is possible, however, that Sthenelaidas was trying to intimidate the Spartiates into making the 'right' decision.

Another democratic element at Sparta was the annual election of five ephors, whose job was to 'oversee' the behaviour of the Spartans and ensure they obeyed the laws. At the beginning of each year the ephors declared war on the helots, and announced that the Spartan citizens should shave their moustaches (see Figure 8 for the 'pseudo-Leonidas' bust which has no moustache). Athenian comedians frequently portrayed Spartans with particularly hairy upper lips, so it seems likely the Spartans often flouted this law and required an annual reminder of the rules. The ephors appear to have come from a broad social spectrum, since Aristotle complained that ephors were corruptible because they were often 'poor'. With five citizens serving as ephors each year, and repeat office apparently unlawful, it is likely that the majority of Spartiates would have served as an ephor during their lifetime, particularly as citizen numbers declined and there were fewer Spartiates available for the role of 'overseeing' the Spartan way of life.

3

The Spartan Lifestyle

Life in Sparta was notoriously hard, so much so that today we use the term 'spartan' to describe something that is plain, unadorned, or lacking in comfort. To illustrate the plainness of Sparta in his day Thucydides (*c.*460–400 BCE) famously (and prophetically) wrote, 'if the city of the Spartans were to become deserted, and only the temples and foundations of building remained' future generations would refuse to believe that Sparta was as powerful as it was, because Sparta had 'no costly temples or edifices', and was simply a collection of villages which made a 'deficient show'. Anyone who has seen the meagre remains of ancient Sparta today would find it hard to disagree!

The Spartan lifestyle was distinctly masculine, and to a considerable extent communal, with Spartiates exercising or hunting together during the day, dining together in the evenings, and some of the young citizens (if not all those aged between 20 and 30) sleeping together in barracks each night. The Spartans' communal lifestyle partly explains why they unusually refused to build defensive fortifications. Of the 1,300 known Greek *poleis* some 526 are known to have had walls, and only four including Sparta are explicitly known to have lacked them; it was only when Sparta was unmistakably too weak to defend itself by manpower alone that they built a wall around the city centre, small sections of which can be seen today. Spartans often dismissed walls as suitable only for women, and two Spartan sayings suggest that the tips of the Spartiates' spears were Sparta's frontier; when a foreigner asked the fourth-century BCE king Agesilaus why Sparta lacked defensive fortifications, he pointed to the citizens under arms and replied smugly, 'These are the Spartans' walls'.

Spartan 'Austerity'

Modern commentators often use the term austerity to describe the Spartan lifestyle because of their reputation for shunning luxury. The Spartan diet was so frugal that a visitor from Sybaris, a luxury-loving Greek city in southern Italy, remarked after sampling it that he no longer considered the Spartans to be genuinely brave, because 'anyone in their right mind would prefer to die ten thousand times than share such a poor living'. Plutarch (*c.*46–120 CE) praises Agesilaus for the fact that the doors on his house were so old and plain they could have been the ones set up when the descendants of Heracles first arrived in Sparta, and reports that when Agesilaus saw rectangular-hewn wooden roof beams in Ionia he asked sarcastically whether trees there grew square, clearly implying that Spartan beams would be unworked logs. Lycurgus was even said to have banned gold and silver currency altogether, requiring the Spartans to use a cumbersome iron currency, weighing approximately 0.6 kg and shaped either like a sacrificial cake or an iron roasting spit. This currency was worthless outside Sparta, useless as base metal because the red-hot iron was quenched in vinegar to make it fragile, and impossible to hoard, with a cartload of around 1,000 kg of iron required to equal the value of 4.3 kg of silver. The Spartans possessed by far the largest economy among the Greek states not minting gold or silver coinage, and their use of iron currency is perhaps not unrelated to the plentiful high-grade iron ore available near the Laconian perioikic community of Boai.

But the austere Spartan lifestyle was not all that it seemed. Although Plutarch claimed that 'luxury atrophied' at Sparta, there were clear signs of wealth to be seen. Some were quite obvious, such as the prominent equestrian culture at Sparta; like today the breeding of racehorses was very much the province of the wealthy in ancient Greece. The Spartans were also regular consumers of decorative art throughout the period from the tenth to the fourth centuries BCE, particularly in ritual contexts. Dedications of black-glazed and red-glazed ceramics, high-quality bronze vessels, mirrors, and statuettes, and lead figurines (Figure 9), have been found in large quantities at Spartan sanctuaries, most notably the sanctuary of Artemis Orthia near the banks of the Eurotas, the temple of Athena Chalkioikos on the Spartan acropolis, the so-called Menelaeum, and the sanctuary of Apollo at Amyclae. There were more subtle signs of wealth at Sparta too. Xenophon (c. 430–354 BCE) reports that 'rich' Spartiates sometimes contributed wheaten bread to the common messes, which would only have been possible for

Figure 9 Archaic period lead figurines from the sanctuary of Artemis Orthia.

those Spartiates who possessed enough land to grow such a prestige crop with a failure rate of 1/4 compared to 1/20 for barley. Xenophon also observes that Spartiates were legally permitted to borrow helots or hunting dogs (provided they invited the owner to the hunt) if they needed them, which indicates that some citizens owned more dogs and helots than others.

But the biggest sham of Spartan 'austerity' was Lycurgus' alleged banning of precious metal coinage. Even if Lycurgus had existed, he could never have banned gold and silver coinage because he was said to have lived either two or four centuries before coinage was ever used in Greece! Many modern experts argue that the formal ban on precious metal coins in Sparta was only a short term arrangement in the late fifth century BCE when vast amounts of silver coinage flooded into Sparta after their victory over Athens in the Peloponnesian War. Until then it was probably not that gold and silver coinage was forbidden at Sparta, but rather that it was not in circulation. Wealthy Spartans would probably have possessed considerable gold and silver, they just could not *spend* it in Sparta itself.

Spartan austerity was probably more about uniformity and conformity than economic restraint, a compromise between the rich and the poor whereby they encouraged the view that the Spartiates were *all* simple soldiers who lived plain lives, shunning luxuries, and had done so for centuries. They even convinced the normally cautious Thucydides that their constitutional arrangements had brought about four centuries of stability. Generations of modern commentators accepted the story too. But it is very unlikely that this was the case, and the latest scholarship dates the start of the stereotypically harsh 'Lycurgan' regime at Sparta to the mid or even late sixth century BCE, barely a generation before Leonidas and his men fought at Thermopylae. Even then Spartan austerity was more about outward displays of wealth rather than the acquisition of it, for Plutarch reveals that Spartiates could keep wealth inside their own home, and various other sources suggest that what went on inside a Spartiate's home was considered his own business. This rather undermines Plutarch's praise of Agesilaus for the plainness of the doors on his house, because Agesilaus could have been the most extravagant Spartan of all time, provided any opulence was kept behind those doors!

Professional Soldiers, or Gentlemen of Leisure?

Many of our surviving primary sources characterize Sparta as a highly militarized society, most obviously Isocrates (436–338 BCE), who claimed that Sparta 'is like a military camp, well administered and rendering willing obedience to officers'. But some experts have started to seriously question the evidence for Spartan military orientation, and with good reason since the *homoioi* spent most of their days engaged not in practising hoplite drill, but in more leisurely pursuits such as gymnastics, ball games, hunting, and generally hanging about with other citizens. In fact, we have no explicit descriptions of the Spartans practising military drill.

However, we need to be careful not to take the notion that Spartan society was not military oriented too far. Indeed, as one recent study put it, 'Sparta's special efficiency in military matters is the one aspect of her history about which we can be most certain'. Although the Spartans spent much time on activities that were 'normal' for wealthy men in other Greek *poleis*, much of their gentlemanly lifestyle—in particular athletics and hunting—would have helped prepare Spartiates for battle. This would have given the Spartans a considerable advantage. For whereas the wealthy citizens of other Greek *poleis* made up just a fraction of the fighting population, every single Spartiate hoplite was a gentleman of leisure who could devote himself to such physical pursuits.

Gymnastic exercises kept Spartiates fit, strong, and agile, and they continued on campaign—hence the vivid image of Leonidas' men exercising naked prior to Thermopylae. Spartans were also famous for their prowess at the *pyrrhichê*, a form of dance in hoplite armour, which Plato (*c.*428–347 BCE) states involved simulating dodging blows and missiles by swerving and ducking, leaping and crouching, as well as offensive postures. Spartan ball games were notoriously brutal, and 'gymnastic' competition in ancient Greece included not only regular athletic events like sprinting, jumping, and throwing, but also sham hoplite combat (the *hoplomachia*), and foot-races in full armour, both of which have obvious military utility. The clear link between sporting prowess and military service at Sparta can be seen in the fact that Spartan Olympic victors were accorded the honour of fighting in the front rank alongside the king, and the (admittedly fragmentary) evidence we possess suggests that the Spartans were particularly successful at Olympic athletic events in the seventh and sixth centuries BCE, at the time of Sparta's greatest territorial expansion.

Hunting would have been useful in conditioning Spartan men and boys to killing with bladed weapons, and the communal element would have helped foster trust—a vital quality in a hoplite phalanx where the shield of the man standing beside you could be the difference between life and death. There was probably also a link between Spartan communal dining and the military, with many modern scholars arguing that two or three dining groups together formed the smallest unit in the Spartan army—the so-called 'sworn band'. Thus the Spartiates who dined together would have sworn to fight alongside each other to the death.

We should also note Xenophon's testimony that the Spartans 'execute very easily manoeuvres that hoplite drill-instructors (*hoplomachoi*) think exceedingly difficult', which surely implies that they practised them. One recent suggestion I find quite attractive is that the Spartans might have deliberately created the impression that they did not practise hoplite drill in order to develop an aura of invincibility.

The Spartiates' primary calling as soldiers can be seen in the fact that only those who died in combat were allowed memorial stones. Some twenty-four small and unadorned inscriptions bearing only the name of the deceased Spartan and the words 'in war' (*en polemôi*) have been found. Unlike other Greeks who typically repatriated combat deaths, the Spartans interred Spartiates who died in combat in a communal grave (*polyandrion*) near the battlefield where they fell, with only with their red cloak and olive leaves. We are fortunate that archaeologists have found one such Spartan *polyandrion* dating to 403 BCE in the Athenian cemetery known as the Kerameikos. The twenty-four skeletons in the 12.4 metre wide tomb are all male, supine, facing east, and were evidently tightly wrapped in cloth at the point of burial, perhaps confirming Plutarch's testimony that Spartiates who fell in battle were buried in their red cloaks. An accompanying inscription records the names of two of the dead—the high-ranking officers Chaeron and Thibrachus—both of whom Xenophon noted were slain and buried at

Athens. Burial abroad like this was a source of pride for the Spartans. When a citizen from Argos tried to mock the Spartans because there were many Spartans buried in Argive territory, a Spartan retorted that there were no Argives buried in Sparta. The implication is clear—the Spartans often invaded Argos, but Argos *never* invaded Sparta.

Plutarch reports that whereas normal Greek practice was to bury the dead outside the city walls (extramural burial), the Spartans were unique in burying their dead—aside from those who died in combat—within the confines of the city. Plutarch claims the Spartans did away with 'superstitious terror' of death to ensure that youths would not be afraid to die in combat. The discovery of numerous burials within the city of Sparta appeared to confirm that image. But the latest archaeological analysis reveals that Spartan burial practices were not as unique as Plutarch suggests. The Spartans actually buried some of their dead outside the city precinct throughout the Archaic, Classical, Hellenistic, and Roman periods, and Argos practised an identical mix of extramural and intramural burial in the same periods. Although some of the graves in and around Sparta are comparatively elaborate, no *stelae* identifying the dead have been found, which does seem to match Plutarch's testimony.

Communal Dining

Spartiates dined together each night in small groups in dedicated mess buildings, which were probably located on the Hyacinthian way, the main thoroughfare between Sparta and Amyclae. Initially called *andreia* ('men's clubs'), but later known as either *philitia* ('friendship clubs'), or *pheiditia* ('thrifty clubs') these dining groups were intended to make the Spartiates more equal, with each citizen required to contribute equal monthly rations of barley, cheese, figs, olive oil, and wine produced locally on his own estates. Aristotle (384–322 BCE) praised the 'democratic' element of requiring all citizens to participate, but criticized Spartan practice as inequitable compared to similar dining clubs in Crete, which were financed by public funds and tithes of the members.

Persaeus of Citium (307–243 BCE) describes Spartiates reclining on shared dining couches (Figure 10), but notes

Figure 10 Bronze figurine of reclining banqueter, *c.*530–500 BCE, British Museum.

that others sat on a 'folding-stool' (*skimpodion*). Given that seven dining couches was standard for a 'modest' Greek dining room, it has been suggested that each Spartan mess comprised fourteen men reclining in pairs on seven couches, plus one man (perhaps the youngest) seated on a stool. The whole setup would have been costly, requiring hundreds of dining rooms, thousands of dining couches and stools, and countless items of tableware. But even in this the Spartans showed characteristic restraint, conspicuously opting for ceramic rather than precious metal plates and drinking cups.

No Spartiate was exempt from this communal experience. The five ephors appear to have had their own mess, and as an equalizing measure even Spartan kings dined in a special royal mess, with each king having two chosen companions called 'Pythians'. The kings were allowed a double portion of food so that they might entertain guests. Spartan kings could on occasion eat at home, and even entertain guests there, but not always. After leading the Spartans to victory at the Battle of Mantinea in 418 BCE, Agis asked for his meal to be delivered to his home so that he could dine with his wife. But the ephors refused him this special treatment, clearly desiring to keep their victorious king's feet firmly on the ground. The next day Agis retaliated by refusing to make a state sacrifice, and in return the ephors fined him for dereliction of duty.

Plutarch says new mess members were screened, with the existing members polled by secret ballot. The vote needed to be unanimous, to ensure that the Spartiates were all 'happy in each other's company'. Given the wealth disparity in

Sparta it seems likely that some messes were more exclusive than others, and it may have been quite clear to poorer Spartans that some messes—like some modern social clubs and fraternities—were not for them.

Xenophon says that Lycurgus' rules ensured that there was enough food to prevent men from either getting too much or too little to eat, and we are told that the ephors fined a certain Naucleides for becoming fat. But the food itself was notoriously bad, so much so that a Spartan saying explained that only those who bathed in the Eurotas River (i.e. native Spartans) could enjoy it. The Spartan dietary staple was barley groats, an unpalatable option for many non-Spartans, more typically consumed by slaves. There was a daily main course (*aiklon*), which consisted of unbaked barley burgers—hence the testimony of Heracleides Lembos (second century BCE) that 'no-one bakes among the Spartans, for they do not harvest wheat, but eat barley'—the notorious 'black broth', also known as 'blood soup' (*haimata*) or 'dipping sauce' (*bapha*), made from pork cooked in salt and blood, and a meat portion. Older Spartiates preferred the blood soup to the meat, perhaps because it was easier for them to eat as their teeth decayed with age. There was also an 'afters' course (*epaiklon*). But this was no dessert course. Indeed, Agesilaus once dismissively 'regifted' sweetmeats to his helots because such extravagances were fitting only for slaves! The *epaiklon* was actually another meat portion, either wild game from hunting expeditions, or lamb or goat from the messmates' flocks. The names of the donors were called aloud so that their 'prowess and assiduity' would be known by all their co-diners.

The Spartans were ostensibly abstemious when it came to their drinking habits, with Xenophon observing that Spartan practice afforded little opportunity for the 'drunken uproar, or coarse actions and words' found at typical Greek drinking parties (*symposia*). Critias (*c.*460–403 BCE) praised the fact that each Spartiate drank from his own cup (the so-called *kôthôn* which had a special lip that trapped the dregs and could also be taken on military campaigns) rather than passing around a wide-mouthed cup (Figure 11) while making elaborate toasts as other Greeks did. Xenophon praises the Spartans for outlawing 'compulsory drinking', and notes that Spartans of military age were obliged to be careful not to

Figure 11 Black-figure Laconian wine cup by the 'Hunt Painter', *c.*550–540 BCE, Antikensammlung, Staatliche Museen zu Berlin.

drink too much because they had to walk home in the dark without the aid of a torch. According to one later story, when some visiting Chians vomited in the hall of the ephors after overindulging in alcohol, the ephors instituted a vigorous investigation to ensure that no Spartiates were responsible. After determining that it must have been the Chians, the ephors issued a retrospective proclamation, 'the Spartans grant permission to the Chians to be filthy'.

However, Spartan dining might not have been quite as restrained as it seems. Modern scholars have calculated that the mess contributions were so large they would have provided each Spartiate with around 6,429 calories per day, as many calories as modern Olympians in training, even *before* he touched the afters course. No wonder then that Xenophon tells us that 'the table is never empty' at Sparta. Various explanations for what happened to this obvious surplus of food have been suggested. One possibility is that the state used the extras to cater for those maintained at public expense –that is, the kings, the Pythians, and the ephors. Another option is that Spartiate mess contributions also supplied the boys undergoing the upbringing. Another suggestion is that the surplus was 'recirculated' back to the helots to feed them and their families. This would have not only limited the portion sizes of the Spartiates, it would also have ensured there was a larger helot population to work on their estates. Another under-explored possibility is the Spartans' other meal of the day, the so-called 'midday meal', which is often mistakenly translated as 'breakfast'. This is not said to have been eaten in common, but there is nothing in our sources to suggest that it could not have been made up from the Spartiates' monthly contributions.

The Spartiates' monthly wine contributions were similarly enormous, equivalent to nearly fifty bottles each per month today. This would have produced a truly astonishing amount of wine when one factors in the standard Greek practice of watering down wine. So if a Spartiate wanted to drink very large quantities only the disapproving eye of his fellow diners would have stopped him. Some clearly did overindulge, for the Spartans even had a special term for drinking stronger wine—'a Scythian cup'—so named because Leonidas' half-brother Cleomenes picked up the habit of drinking neat wine from Scythian ambassadors to Sparta. Even then a drunkard's fellow diners might hide his indiscretions; Plutarch tells us that each night the eldest member of the mess pointed to the doors and reminded his fellow diners, 'not a word goes out through these'.

Spartan Piety

Herodotus (c.484–425 BCE) reports that the Spartans were so devoted to the gods that 'divine matters took precedence over human ones'. Like all ancient Greeks the Spartans were polytheistic, worshipping the standard Greek deities, for example Zeus, Poseidon, Apollo, Athena, and Artemis amongst many. The Spartans appear to have been particularly devoted to Apollo, with three major annual festivals in his honour: the Hyacinthia (May/June), the Gymnopaidiai (July), and the Carneia (August). As is often the case with

Sparta there were peculiarities; they worshipped Helen of Troy—formerly the queen of Sparta—and her estranged husband Menelaus, as well as Lycurgus the lawgiver. Moreover, all their deities were depicted armed, with even Aphrodite the goddess of love said to have put aside her 'magical girdle' and donned armour to please Lycurgus. But none of this was quite as peculiar as it is often presented; other Greeks worshipped their own local deities, and the travel-writer Pausanias (c.110–180 CE) reported seeing armed statues of Aphrodite in Corinth and Epidaurus.

Nonetheless, the Spartans' reputation for hyper-piety is borne out in numerous stories of earthquakes being enough to stop a Spartan army in its tracks because it was seen as a sign that Poseidon 'the Earth-shaker' disapproved of their campaign. The Spartans believed that a devastating earthquake that struck Sparta c.464 BCE was caused by their sacrilegious execution of helots who had sought sanctuary at Poseidon's temple at Cape Taenarum in Laconia. Spartans were notorious for needing to consult the gods before making *any* major decision. As we have already seen Lycurgus reputedly had the Spartan constitution endorsed by Apollo, and when the Spartans went to war against the Athenians in the Peloponnesian War they did so only after consulting Apollo and learning that he would support them, even though they already firmly believed that the Athenians had impiously broken a sworn peace treaty with them. Even with Apollo's explicit support, Thucydides reports that when the war went against them the Spartans assumed that this was because they had acted impiously by not accepting an Athenian offer of arbitration, which was a stipulation of the sworn peace treaty they accused the Athenians of breaking in the first place.

Herodotus reports that the Spartans panicked when they began receiving bad omens from the gods after they impiously killed ambassadors sent by Xerxes' father Darius. Two Spartans, Sperthias and Bulis, responded to a call from the ephors for volunteers to sacrifice themselves to atone for the impiety. Sperthias and Bulis travelled all the way to Xerxes' court at Susa, where they caused great offence by refusing to follow Persian court protocol by prostrating themselves before the king. Sperthias and Bulis were not just being difficult; they felt that it would be impious to prostrate themselves before a mere mortal. But Xerxes refused to kill them, clearly judging correctly that it was crueller not to release the overly-superstitious Spartans from their guilt.

Spartan religious festivals allowed the Spartans a rare opportunity to indulge themselves while they were worshipping. There were special feasts known as a 'Cleaver' (*kopis*)—a nod towards the meat that was consumed there—at which Spartiates could partake of more exotic food than normal, such as wheaten bread and pastries. They do not seem to have been required to dine in messes, and could even entertain foreign guests. The fact that Xenophon praised Agesilaus for how frugally he feasted on festival days implies strongly that other Spartans showed no such restraint when normal dining rules did not apply.

The Hyacinthia festival, which started out as a sombre affair as the Spartans mourned for Apollo's dead lover Hyacinthus, transformed into a bustling celebration with sacrifices, feasting, and even the entertainment of foreign guests. Boys played the kithara (a type of lyre) and sang to pipe music, others rode horses through the theatre, and there were choral performances. Everyone was treated to the spectacle of unmarried girls driving elaborately tricked out carts and racing chariots as the entire populace processed to Amyclae, emptying the city of Sparta itself. Another festival honouring Apollo noted for its pomp and ceremony was the Gymnopaidiai. Meaning either the festival of 'the naked boys' or 'the unarmed dancers', this festival was named after a gruelling day-long competition between naked choruses of boys and mature men in the baking summer heat. The Spartans clearly threw themselves into this festival, with Pausanias reporting that 'if there is one festival the Spartans celebrate with their heart and soul it is the Gymnopaidiai'. One of the highlights of Spartan religious festivals was the so-called *trichoria* (literally 'the three choruses'), when the old men would sing, 'we were once valiant young men', after which the men in their prime would respond, 'But we are the valiant ones now; put us to the test, if you wish', to which the boys replied, 'But we shall be far mightier'. Even the lame king Agesilaus took part in such choruses, but he was apparently kept at the back where no one could see his flawed body clearly.

Although music and dance was such a key part of Spartan religious activity that the dramatist Pratinas of Phlius (*c.*500 BCE) wrote 'the cicada is Spartan, eager for a chorus', the Spartans developed a reputation for demeaning musical proficiency. Aristotle criticized the Spartans for stigmatizing learning to play musical instruments as 'slavish', and after listening to a professional harpist the exiled king Demaratus reputedly remarked 'To me it's just foolery, but he does it pretty well'. This suggests that the Spartans despised musical professionalism, with Demaratus' comment meaning not that playing music was inherently unimportant to Spartans, but that learning to play *that well* was a waste of time.

Spartan Xenophobia

The Spartans appear to have been particularly troubled by the threat outsiders represented to their austere lifestyle. Plato tells us that young Spartan men were not allowed to travel abroad, 'lest they unlearn what they are taught at home', and Isocrates suggests that this restriction on movement extended to all Spartan adults fit for military service (i.e. men aged 20–60). The Spartans also routinely banished foreigners from Sparta altogether, a practice known as *xenêlasia* (sometimes translated as 'alien act'). Herodotus provides good examples of this practice. When a rich Samian tried to bribe Leonidas' half-brother Cleomenes, he went straight to the ephors and told them to order the foreigner to leave Sparta. On another occasion, when Aristagoras the tyrant of Miletus tried to bribe the same Cleomenes to assist the Ionian Greeks in their revolt against the Persians, Cleomenes' 8-year-old daughter Gorgo urged him to kick the 'little foreigner' out before he was corrupted by him. In a wonderful piece of theatre Cleomenes obeys his daughter and runs out of the room to avoid temptation.

Spartans were frequently rude to outsiders. Thucydides reports that the Spartans flat-out refused to tell him how many Spartans died at the Battle of Mantinea in 418 BCE.

When Agis, the victor at Mantinea, was once asked what reply an ambassador should take back home he replied merely, 'That you spoke and I listened'. Agis' half-brother Agesilaus rudely rebuffed the world-famous Athenian tragic actor Callippides. When the stunned thespian responded 'Do you not recognize me?', Agesilaus replied insultingly, 'Are you not Callippides the *deikêliktas*?', thus dismissing an accomplished professional as a lowbrow comedy mime actor. When Timotheus of Miletus, a famous practitioner of 'new music', travelled to Sparta to compete at a festival, the Spartan ephors are said to have cut off the 'extra' two strings from his innovative new lyre, shouting 'Don't do harm to music!'

Rudeness aside, these episodes show Spartans engaging in typical Greek interstate activities. The Spartans received foreign ambassadors, athletes and musicians travelled to Sparta to participate at religious festivals, and Spartiates acted as *proxenoi*, a hereditary role whereby private citizens represented the interests of another state in their own city. Spartans also travelled abroad, where foreigners acted as *proxenoi* for them, most notably the fifth-century BCE Athenian statesman Alcibiades, who made himself available to the captives who surrendered at Sphacteria. The Spartans even headed a complex international alliance system, which modern scholars call the 'Peloponnesian League'.

The Spartans were not as indifferent to outside tastes as many of these stories suggest. In the sixth century BCE Laconian workshops produced high-quality black-glazed ceramic vessels (see Figure 11), which were heavily influenced by eastern artistic styles, and widely exported, especially to Samos off the coast of Asia Minor and Etruria in central Italy. The decline of these Laconian workshops in the late sixth century BCE is often linked to Spartan austerity, but the connection is by no means clear-cut. The success of Laconian black-glazed pottery abroad appears to have depended on only a handful of artists, which might explain why their success was so comparatively short-lived. The decline might also be linked to changes in tastes, with the Etruscans turning their attention to decorated pottery from Athens. Furthermore, although Laconian exports declined, Laconian workshops continued to produce black-glazed and red-glazed pottery for internal use throughout the Classical period, and in the period between 420 and 370 BCE Laconian workshops produced pottery that essentially imitated Athenian red-figure styles.

But perhaps the best illustration of Spartan attitudes to outsiders comes from just before the outbreak of the Peloponnesian War (431–404 BCE), when the Spartans demanded that the Athenians stop punishing their allies from Megara by denying them access to the markets of the cities across Athens' Aegean-wide empire. The Athenians responded that they would open their markets to Megarians provided the Spartans opened the marketplace in Sparta to them. The Spartans refused the offer, suggesting that they feared the taint of the outside world enough that they were willing to risk going to war to avoid it.

Spartan Duplicity

The Spartans' secrecy and indifference to outsiders went hand-in-glove with their reputation for deceit. The chorus of Athenian farmers in Aristophanes' comedy *Peace* (421 BCE) derides the Spartans as 'children of foxes, their heads treacherous, their minds treacherous', and the chorus of old men in Aristophanes' *Acharnians* (425 BCE) complains that for Spartans 'neither sanctity, nor pledge, nor oath holds true'. But we need to show some caution here, for most of the negative comments about Spartan duplicity come from Athenian commentators. A good illustration of the perils of taking the Athenians' word for Spartan deceit is Herodotus' testimony that when Leonidas' nephew Pausanias gave orders to the allied Greek army to withdraw prior to the Battle of Plataea in 479 BCE because the Persians had disrupted their water supply, the Athenian troops alone refused to move, 'well knowing that the Spartans would think one thing but say another'. But the Spartans were not indulging in a stratagem as the Athenians thought; Pausanias really did want the army to withdraw. So the Spartans were not always as tricky as the Athenians thought.

Nonetheless, some Spartans clearly revelled in their reputation as tricksters, and one modern expert has even suggested that the 'right to lie' was a badge of status for Spartiates. Agesilaus claimed that 'to outwit the enemy is not only right and reputable, but also pleasant and profitable'. Agesilaus may have learned a thing or two about trickery from his mentor Lysander, who claimed, 'sometimes the lion skin must be pieced out with that of the fox', when criticized for indulging in too much trickery. Their contemporary Dercylidas had such a reputation for deception that he was nicknamed 'Sisyphus' after the mythical king of Corinth who cheated death by persuading the god of the Underworld to allow him to return to earth briefly to remonstrate with his wife. Once back on *terra firma* Sisyphus defaulted on the bargain and lived out a long second life!

Perhaps the most revealing act of Spartan trickery was that which Cleomenes committed against the Argives in 494 BCE. Herodotus reports that the Argives tried to avoid a battle with Cleomenes by copying whatever signal he gave to his herald. When Cleomenes realized this he gave orders that when the Spartan herald announced the midday meal the Spartans should instead don their armour and attack. The trick worked with the Spartans catching the Argives totally unprepared, and slaughtering them in their thousands. When the Argive survivors fled into a grove sacred to the hero Argus, Cleomenes lured around fifty out one-by-one with false promises of ransom, and killed them. But when the rest realized what was happening and refused to come out, Cleomenes was so frustrated that he burned the grove to the ground to prevent them from escaping. Some Spartans could be brutal as well as deceptive.

Spartan Misbehaviour

All the secrecy and lying hid an inconvenient truth—Spartans were not always obedient to the law, and did not always use deceit within acceptable limits. In fact, the Spartans developed a particularly poor reputation for rule-breaking when abroad. A prime example is Cleomenes, whose acts of sacrilege abroad were truly stunning. Not only did he burn Argus' sacred grove (although technically he made his helots do it), Cleomenes also bribed the oracle at Delphi to say that his co-king Demaratus was illegitimate, flogged the priest at the Argive Heraion (again ordering his helots to do it), and defiled a precinct sacred to Demeter and Persephone at Eleusis in Athenian territory. He also dug up the remains of the Athenian noble family the Alcmaeonidae, and desecrated the remains of the Argive hero Anthes, allegedly flaying the skin from his rotting corpse to make vellum for transcribing oracles. Back at home Cleomenes took to poking Spartiates with his staff, and was accused of plotting with Sparta's neighbours in Arcadia and even the helots. Cleomenes ended up in chains, but he bullied the helot who was guarding him into giving him a knife; he then hacked himself to death with the knife, slashing his shins, thighs, and finally his belly; a truly gruesome end for a brutal man who stretched the rules beyond breaking point.

Cleomenes' nephew Pausanias, who briefly led a Greek coalition which aimed to liberate the Greeks of Asia from Persian rule after the repulse of Xerxes' invasion forces, also went astray overseas. Pausanias, who at home in Greece mocked the Persians for their love of luxury, took to wearing Persian trousers once abroad, travelled around with a bodyguard of Persians and Egyptians, tried to seduce all the pretty girls in Byzantium (stabbing one to death when she startled him by sneaking into his bed in the dark), and generally offended all the other Greeks with his violent temper. He was even alleged to have written to Xerxes offering to make Sparta and Greece subject to Persia. Due to his misbehaviour, Pausanias was recalled to Sparta, but soon after his return he was accused of scheming at revolution with the helots. Even then the ephors were slow to act against him, partly because they did not trust the word of the helots. But when Pausanias was denounced by his ex-boyfriend who provided written proof in the form of a letter Pausanias sent to the Persians with orders to kill the messenger, the ephors finally resolved to act. But when they tried to arrest Pausanias, he fled and took sanctuary in the temple of Athena Chalkioikos. The ephors shut him in until he collapsed from hunger, and then they dragged him out just before he died, thus (technically) avoiding polluting the temple. Thucydides reports that the Spartans intended to throw his body into the gorge called Kaiadas, where the Spartans cast 'malefactors', but decided to bury him nearby, which was fortunate, for soon afterwards the oracle of Delphi ordered them to reinter him at Athena's sacred precinct.

Probably the most telling example of a Spartan behaving badly abroad is Gylippus, who had hitherto been such an exemplary Spartan that the general Lysander entrusted him with the task of delivering to Sparta vast numbers of sacks of money plundered after capturing Athens in 404 BCE. Gylippus betrayed Lysander's trust, stealing large amounts of silver—allegedly 180,000 drachmas, at least 45,000 silver coins—from the bottom of each sack and hiding the cash under the roof-tiles of his house. Gylippus then delivered the seemingly pristine sacks to the ephors. But Gylippus was unaware that the crafty Lysander had placed a note at the top of each sack indicating the exact sum inside. So when the ephors counted the money they found that it did not tally with Lysander's notes. The discrepancy perplexed them, until one of Gylippus' helots told them Gylippus had 'many owls sleeping under his roof-tiles', an enigmatic reference to the fact that Athenian silver coins bore an image of an owl. After Gylippus' disgrace the ephors took action against the dangers presented by this influx of wealth, temporarily banning gold and silver coinage from Sparta altogether.

The Spartan Double Life?

In recent years there has been a trend amongst academics to question much of what we are told about the Spartans' distinctive lifestyle. In particular, scholars have started homing in on the fact that many of the stories of Spartan uniqueness are negative stereotypes put forward by the Athenians, such as the Athenian statesman Pericles' portrayal of the Spartans as xenophobic and militarized in his 'Funeral Oration' of 431 BCE. Thucydides reports that Pericles contrasted how the Athenians threw their city open to the world with the Spartans' practice of *xenêlasia* which prevented foreigners from hearing or observing what they did. Pericles also reportedly claimed that Athenians were 'naturally brave' whereas Spartans needed to have courage beaten into them during their brutal upbringing. The realization that we are so frequently dealing with negative stereotypes has led some experts to ask whether most of the claims that the Spartans were radically different are just part of the Spartan mirage, and that the Spartans were not really that different after all.

But the danger with this line of thought is that it treats the Spartan mirage almost like a 'get-out clause' that permits us to explain away aspects of Spartan life that seem too unusual. My own view is that if the Spartans really were quite normal the 'mirage' would never have developed in the first place. The Spartans' secrecy, lying, and expulsion of outsiders shows us not only that they behaved differently to other Greeks, but also that they wanted to keep aspects of their way of life away from prying eyes. It should also be borne in mind that 'negative' stereotypes are not by default untrue, and are not always (if at all) viewed as negative by the people being stereotyped as such. Just because the Athenians thought that Spartan rigid obedience was a bad thing does not necessarily mean Spartans themselves felt the same. After all, in today's society many people see strict obedience to rules as a bad thing, but few serving in the armed forces or living in closed communities would agree.

Rather than seeing the Spartans as more normal than we used to think, it would be better to see them as leading what one academic recently called a 'double life', whereby they had more freedom to acquire wealth and in their private lives than we thought, but at the same time they were subject to restrictions on conspicuous displays of wealth and how they conducted their lives in public when compared to other Greek cities. Certainly, we must accept that Sparta was not as 'austere' as outsiders painted it, but we should not allow our recognition of that fact to overshadow the fact that so many Greek writers saw the Spartan lifestyle as very different to their own.

4

Raising a Spartan

Spartans were raised to be tough. To illustrate this Plutarch (*c*.46–120 CE) told the story of a Spartan boy who stole a fox cub, and in order to escape detection, hid it in his cloak. When the fox turned 'savage', the boy remained steadfastly silent while his insides were clawed and bitten out, rather than cry out and be caught stealing. Although this tale sounds fanciful, Plutarch says he believes it because he himself saw 'many' Spartan youths dying during a ritual flogging at the altar of Artemis Orthia.

But while the story of the boy and the fox cub creates a vivid image of the harshness of Spartan childhood, many modern scholars dismiss it as a later invention born out of Sparta's reputation for toughness. Some doubt the story because Plutarch is the only source to mention it. Others have questioned why a boy might 'steal' a fox. But as odd as it might sound to us, foxes were eaten regularly in ancient Greece, with Galen (119–*c*.200 CE) reporting that they were an autumn delicacy for Greek hunters, as the foxes had grown fat on fallen grapes. It is also important to note that the vast majority of stories Plutarch tells about the Spartan upbringing match the testimony of earlier writers like Xenophon (*c.*430–354 BCE), Plato (*c.*428–347 BCE), and Isocrates (436–338 BCE). So when attempting to determine what we can and cannot say about the Spartan upbringing we need to make sure that we are not being too sceptical about later sources like Plutarch.

Spartan Eugenics?

The process of raising Spartans began even before they were conceived. Xenophon observes that whereas girls in other Greek cities performed seated indoor tasks like weaving, Spartan girls were compelled to exercise outside, in the belief that 'strapping' babies would be produced if both parents were physically strong. Xenophon also reveals that Spartan men were discouraged from sleeping with their wives whenever they wished, in the belief that too much sex would leave men exhausted and unable to conceive 'sturdy' offspring.

Plutarch reports that new-born Spartan babies were inspected by the eldest men in the tribe, who immersed them in unmixed wine to test their reactions. If they were weak or disabled, they were cast into a 'precipitous spot' near Mt Taygetus known as Apothetae (from the Greek *apotithêmi*, 'to put away'). A cleft in the Taygetus range at Parori, west of modern Sparti, and a cave at Trypi ('Hole') have both been identified as possible locations for the dumping ground for rejected Spartan infants, and the Kaiadas gorge where Spartans disposed of criminals. But as this notorious practice is mentioned only by Plutarch, some modern experts dismiss it as a late invention projected onto earlier Spartan practice. But even if this is the case, we should not be lulled into thinking that the Spartans would have normally allowed disabled babies to be reared. The harsh reality is that parents exposed unwanted children throughout the ancient Greek world. The decision to raise the lame Agesilaus was surely the exception rather than the rule at Sparta, and it is possible that he survived because his disability, which was insufficient to prevent him from completing the upbringing, was not immediately obvious.

Organizing the Upbringing

Spartan education was unique in the ancient world, in being both organized by the state and compulsory for all citizens. Xenophon explicitly contrasted the compulsory state-run Spartan system with other Greek cities where children were entrusted to slave tutors and private teachers, and Aristotle (384–322 BCE)—normally no fan of Sparta—praised the fact that at Sparta the sons of the rich and poor were raised in identical manner. Only the immediate heirs to the two Spartan thrones were exempt from what Plutarch calls 'training in obeying rules'.

The Spartan upbringing may have been called the *agôgê* (from the Greek *agein*, 'to lead'), a term which, one modern expert observed, 'denotes a mixture of upbringing and training'. But that name appears no earlier than the middle of the third century BCE, and even then in quotations by later Roman writers. Contemporary sources like Xenophon use the generic Greek term for education—*paideia*—when describing the Spartan upbringing, although Plato does use the term *agôgê* when describing education in general.

The Spartan state appointed an official to manage this brutal process. His title—*paidonomos*—meant rather ominously 'boy-herder', which is perhaps linked to the separation of boys into 'herds' at age 7. But again the facts are confused. Three terms for groupings of boys appear in our sources: *agelai*, *bouai*, and *ilai*. The first is a generic Greek term for 'herd', the second a term derived from the Greek word for cattle, and the third—used by our earliest sources—is a technical military term similar to our 'squadron'. Only *bouai* seems uniquely Spartan, but it appears in our sources only very late. We can therefore conclude only that Spartan boys were divided into groups, and that they came to be known as 'herds' by the Roman period at the latest.

We can state confidently that there were three stages to the Spartan education process. It started around age 7, when Spartan boys were known collectively as just that—'boys' (*paides*). Around age 14 the boys became *paidiskoi*, usually translated as 'youths', but literally meaning 'little boys', a neat way of keeping Spartan teenagers in their place. At age 20 Spartan youths became *hêbôntes* ('young men in their prime'), but even though these young Spartan adults were now citizens required to join a mess and serve in the army, the testing and monitoring continued. Only when Spartan males reached the age of 30 could their education be said to be complete. Xenophon lauds this three-part system as ensuring that 'respect and obedience in combination are found to a high degree at Sparta'.

Discipline and Punishment

The behaviour of Spartan boys and youths was strictly controlled and they were under constant observation. If the *paidonomos* was not present any available ordinary citizen would watch over the boys, and failing that, one of the cleverest of the *eirênes* (probably young men aged 20) would step in. Xenophon concludes—rather ominously I think—'boys at Sparta are never without someone in charge of them'.

Spartan boys were not merely watched. To ensure that they behaved properly the *paidonomos* was supported by a staff of *hêbôntes* called the 'whip-bearers' (*mastigophoroi*). Any infractions were met with beatings, which must have been brutal considering Spartan whips were probably much more like a bullwhip than a cat-o'-nine-tails. If a Spartan father learned that his son had been flogged, he too would issue a further beating, which is unlikely to have been a minor matter given that the Spartans developed a nasty reputation for striking out with their staffs. Corporal punishment was so integral to the boys' upbringing that Plato claimed the Spartans taught 'not by persuasion but by violence', and one modern scholar recently suggested every Spartan would have endured at least twenty years of being hit by other Spartans.

This violent enforcement of Spartan norms partly explains why they were famous for the respect that they showed for their elders. Herodotus (*c*.484–425 BCE) tells us that the Spartans were unique amongst the Greeks in that younger men would stand aside or rise from their seats when their elders approached. To illustrate this behaviour Plutarch tells a wonderful (almost certainly fictional) tale of Spartan delegates in Athens for the Panathenaea games watching on with horror as the Athenians mocked and tormented an old man who could not find a seat. When the Spartans to a man rose to offer him their seats in the front row—the ancient equivalent of the corporate boxes at modern stadiums—the Athenians applauded to show their approval. The Spartans then responded with the smug put down, 'By the twin gods, the Athenians know what is the right thing to do, but do not do it!'

There were strict rules regarding Spartan boys' appearance. Their hair was kept shorn and they were restricted to one cloak. Xenophon says Spartan boys were even denied shoes to ensure that they would be able to 'jump and bound and run faster than those with shoes'. Together with the sickle (*xuêlê*) they carried as a makeshift woodcutter and bath scraper (like a Spartan one-bladed Swiss Army knife) their appearance would have served as a kind of uniform distinguishing them not only from the long-haired and red-cloaked adults, but also the helots, who wore dog-skin caps and leather jerkins. Their sickles could be dangerous— Xenophon describes meeting a 'Spartiate' named Dracontius who was exiled while still a boy (*pais*) because he accidentally killed another boy with a blow from his *xuêlê*.

Xenophon reports that their diet was strictly controlled to ensure that boys did not become sluggish by being too full, and to give them a taste of what it is like to not have enough. Xenophon stresses that their meagre rations were 'plain', and later sources confirm that Spartan boys were denied the 'black broth' so beloved by adults. Instead, their main meal comprised barley burgers, with an 'afters' course of more barley burgers. The theory behind their frugal diet was that it would produce tall, slim bodies, and the ephors are said to have inspected the young men naked every ten days to ensure that they remained slim.

Plutarch says that the 'smartest' of the *eirênes* took command of the boys' herds, and oversaw their food gathering activities. The boys would then serve the *eirên* his own meal. On occasion the *eirên* would also ask the boys questions, biting them on the thumb to punish wrong answers. The *eirênes* might also chastise the boys in the presence of elders and officials. Plutarch claims that on such occasions the decisions the *eirên* made were accepted without interference, but after the boys were dismissed the *eirên* would be forced to account for any punishment that was deemed unduly harsh or soft.

Plutarch also says that Spartan boys slept together in their herds, on mattresses they made themselves by pulling reeds from the banks of the Eurotas with their bare hands. In winter they were allowed to mix thistledown into the mattresses, in the belief that this would emanate warmth. This aspect of their lives sounds particularly harsh, and some experts suggest this was not normal practice in pre-Roman Sparta, but rather something that happened only occasionally as part of the boys' endurance training.

Sometimes Spartan boys would attend the adult common messes. This was not for eating; Xenophon reports that the boys would be questioned by their elders, while Plutarch notes that they would hear political discussions and witness the kind of entertainments that would be appropriate when they too became citizens. These included making fun without being indecent, and not taking offence when they were the butt of a joke. Plutarch says 'the ability to take a joke would seem to be very Spartan', and Sosibius (third century BCE) describes Spartan dinner-time jesting as 'seasoning for the drudgery of their way of life'.

Xenophon claims their meagre diet forced Spartan boys to steal to ward off starvation, and Plutarch describes them hunting in teams, targeting the adults' mess halls and gardens near the city, with older boys doing the stealing while the youngsters acted as lookouts. Unsurprisingly, the ever-present whip was used on any boys caught in the act. But Xenophon explains this was not because they had been stealing—since they were actually encouraged to steal—but rather to teach them to become better thieves. Although modern scholars often struggle to rationalize this practice, Xenophon reports that Spartan larceny training had a military function, because a prospective thief must keep awake at night, lie in wait during the day, and keep spies ready, thus making Spartans more resourceful and better fighters in the long term.

When Spartan boys grew into youths (*paidiskoi*), their training and monitoring became more intense. Xenophon states that because youths are 'self-willed' and 'prone to cockiness' the Spartans 'loaded them with work' to keep them 'occupied for the maximum time'. Xenophon also stresses the rigidity of their required behaviour: in the streets *paidiskoi* had to keep their hands within their cloak, proceed in silence, and not let their gaze wander, but instead keep it fixed on the ground. In a wonderful analogy Xenophon states that one would have more chance of catching the eye of a bronze statue than a Spartan youth! Lapses were now more serious, and could even lead to complete dishonour, rather like a recruit in the modern military failing to complete basic training.

Flagellation remained a key part of the youths' upbringing, most obviously in the notorious and bloody cheesestealing ceremony in honour of the goddess Artemis Orthia. Our Classical-period sources are quite vague about what happened at her temple near the banks of the Eurotas River. The most detailed testimony we have is Xenophon's observation that it was 'a matter of honour' for Spartan youths to snatch as many cheeses as possible from Orthia's altar while others whipped them. Plato must be referring to this when he talks of 'certain acts of theft which take place amid a constant hail of blows'. But we can really only say with confidence that in Xenophon's time Spartan youths stole cheeses and were whipped while they did so.

We know far more about the Roman-period version of this rite of passage which appears to have been transformed into a daylong extravaganza called the 'Flagellation' (*diamastigô-sis*), a full-blown feat of endurance—minus the cheese stealing—with boys seeking the prize for withstanding the most beatings. Both Plutarch and Cicero (106–43 BCE) witnessed Spartan boys dying under the lash, with Cicero claiming the boys endured their fatal beating in silence. But there is no hint of such extreme performances for tourists in earlier times.

A Sporting Life

The need to develop sturdy bodies combined with a desire to keep the youths occupied meant that a considerable part of Spartan education involved bodily exercises. Spartan youths practised running, wrestling, jumping, throwing (both javelin and discus), and perhaps also boxing and the brutal *pankration* (a mix of boxing and wrestling). There is some doubt about the latter two sports because later tradition had it that the Spartans shunned them because it was possible to yield and they did not want to encourage boys to think that it was acceptable to give up. If Spartan boys were wealthy enough to own horses they might also participate in equestrian sports.

While the Spartans may have avoided boxing and the *pankration*, this does not mean that they were shy about hitting each other. Plato mentions 'group fights with bare knuckles', and some modern scholars see this as a reference to a ritual bare-knuckle fight that Pausanias (*c.*110–180 CE) says took place in a sacred grove surrounded by a moat. According to Pausanias, after sacrificing a puppy to the war-god Enyalios, two teams of Spartan boys entered the grove and tried to drive their opponents into the water by punching, biting, and gouging.

Spartan boys took part in a variety of other sporting competitions. We are fortunate to have a large dedication to Athena from shortly after 400 BCE which commemorates victories by a certain Damonon and his son Enymacratidas at various local religious festivals. The stele records Damonon's victories in the one stade sprint (approximately 185 metres) and the two stade sprint, and Enymacratidas' clearly remark-able victories in the boys' stade sprint, two stade sprint, the long foot race, and the race on horseback all on the same day at the Parparonia festival. There were also special sporting competitions for the boys associated with the cult of Artemis Orthia which may have been the context of the cheese-stealing ritual. A fourth-century BCE inscription atop a dedi-cation of five sickles commemorating one youth's successes reads: 'Victorious Arexippus dedicated these to Orthia, manifest for all to see in the gatherings of boys'. Such dedi-cations became standard practice in the Hellenistic and Roman periods as sporting competitions in honour of Arte-mis evolved into a final rite of passage as the boys transi-tioned into adulthood.

Spartan youths will also have played team ball sports. Xenophon speaks of Spartan adults playing ball games, and in the Hellenistic period Spartan youths played a game called *sphairomachia* ('battle-ball'). This game was probably the same one known elsewhere in Greece as *episkyros*, a form of 'force 'em back' in which teams vied to catch a ball and throw it over the opposing team until one pushed the other over a back line. This game has been described as 'like a hybrid of North American football, rugby, and a sort of netless volleyball', and would have required a combination of agility, co-operation, and mass strength. By the Roman period this game had become so synonymous with Sparta that the writer Lucian (*c.*125–180 CE) warned a protégé travelling to Sparta, 'Remember not to laugh at them . . . when they charge and strike one another over a ball in the theatre'.

Reading, Writing, and Arithmetic?

Outsiders often alleged that the Spartans were unschooled academically. The Athenian Isocrates claimed that the Spartans 'do not even learn their letters', while Hippias of Elis (a famous fifth-century BCE sophist) said 'many of them do not know how to count'. Because of these early criticisms Plutarch's claim that 'Spartan boys learned to read and write no more than was necessary' is sometimes taken as implying that the Spartans could barely read and write at all. But we need to bear in mind that Isocrates' claims were part of a mendacious diatribe against Sparta intended to show Athenian superiority, and Hippias was aggrieved that the Spartans rejected his offers to teach their youngsters for a fee. It may be simply that the Spartans had a rather different view about what was 'necessary', because Sparta was a society where written expression was very much secondary to oral expression.

There are in fact strong grounds for thinking that the majority of the Spartans did learn to read and write. Some stone inscriptions survive from the Classical period. Admittedly there are not many, but there are not really any fewer than survive from the majority of ancient Greek cities. If most Spartans could not read, why would the likes of Arexippus and Damonon have bothered to have their sporting achievements written down on stone? Secondly, officials such as the ephors were required to be able to write, and, as we have seen already, every single Spartiate had a genuine chance to serve as an ephor. The ephors wrote messages to military commanders using a coded message stick called a *skytalê*. Commanders would be expected to write back too. We are fortunate that one such message has been recorded by Xenophon: 'Ships lost, Mindarus dead, don't know what to do'. These words written by a desperate second-in-command after a disastrous naval defeat were necessarily very brief, but the junior officer was clearly capable of writing.

Some modern experts argue that it would have been customary for wealthier Spartan fathers who wanted their sons to be more literate to supplement the meagre state tuition by organizing private tuition from specialist teachers like Hippias of Elis. But this notion clashes outright with Aristotle's claim that the sons of the rich and poor Spartans were raised in identical manner, and Xenophon's emphatic statement that whereas other Greeks entrusted their children to private teachers, Spartans entrusted their sons to a state official. The idea that foreign experts might be paid to teach at Sparta is further undermined by Hippias' own testimony (quoted by Plato) that 'it is not lawful for Spartans to provide their youths with a foreign education'. That only a very small minority of Spartans attained higher levels of literacy seems likely given the only known Classical-period prose writers Sparta produced were members of the social elite; the Spartan king Pausanias wrote a treatise on Lycurgus, and the general Thibron wrote a history. Both works are lost.

Laconic Speech

The philosopher Heracleides (390–310 BCE) observed that 'from childhood Spartans are taught to speak briefly'. This Spartan practice of using as few words as possible is

the origin of the English term 'laconic'. The Spartans' lin-
guistic austerity was not a sign of intellectual poverty. Plutarch describes Spartan brevity as both 'profound' and
'graceful', while Socrates observed, with obvious admiration, that if you choose to speak to an ordinary Spartan at
first you will find him simple in words, 'But then he throws
up valuable words short and terse like a javelin, so that you
will seem no better than a child'. Furthermore, the sixth-
century BCE Spartan ephor Chilon, who was famous for his
terse aphorisms such as 'honour old age', 'obey the laws',
and 'do not desire what is impossible', was recognized as one
of the so-called 'Seven Sages' of ancient Greece. But Thucydides' backhanded compliment that the fifth-century BCE
Spartan general Brasidas 'was not incapable as a speaker, for
a Lacedaemonian' suggests that some outsiders thought that
Spartan brevity lacked eloquence.

Many memorable one-liners by Spartans were gathered
together in a work attributed to Plutarch known as the
Laconica apophthegmata ('Laconian sayings'). A common
theme in these sayings is the blunt Spartan dismissal of
foreigners' speeches as overly wordy, such as the fourth-
century BCE king Agesilaus' response to someone praising
an orator for his ability to magnify small points: 'It's not a
good cobbler who fits large shoes on small feet'. Although
many of the sayings in the *Laconica apophthegmata* are of
questionable historical reliability, several preserved by earlier sources have an impeccable pedigree. One is Thucydides'
quotation of the ephor Sthenelaidas' blunt response to
Athenian ambassadors: 'these long speeches of the Athenians I do not understand'. The other is Herodotus' report of

the withering Spartan response to a long and impassioned speech requesting their assistance by envoys from Samos. After the verbose Samians finished speaking the Spartan ephors responded that the Samians had spoken so long that they had forgotten the beginning of their speech and therefore did not understand the end. Spartan brevity may even be reflected in Homer's *Iliad* where Menelaus is described as using 'few words, but very clearly cut'.

Brevity of speech has been described as Sparta's own form of rhetoric, designed not only to be intelligent, but ultimately unanswerable. Perhaps the best example of this is Dieneces' famous one-liner, 'we'll fight in the shade'. As one modern scholar recently put it, for Spartans 'actions were what mattered, not speech making'.

Spartan Pederasty

A central part of a Spartan youth's education was mentoring by an older male. In Sparta the boy's mentor was known as the *eispnêlas* ('inspirer'). But he was not mentoring in the modern sense. What we are talking about here is the Spartan version of the traditional ancient Greek practice of 'pederasty', a homoerotic relationship between a pubescent boy and an adult male. Elsewhere in the Greek world the elder partner in a pederastic relationship was known as the *erastês* ('the one who loves'), while the younger was known as the *erômenos* ('the one who is loved'). These terms have often been interpreted by modern scholars as implying that the older male played the active sexual role in anal intercourse, and the younger boy the passive. But this is by no means clear, and many modern experts suggest that pederastic partners were more likely to engage in intercrural sex.

Rather problematically for us, Xenophon is at pains to point out that Spartan pederastic unions were not sexual, and that Spartans actually considered sexual molestation of boys as unacceptable as incest. Xenophon describes the Spartans as taking the middle ground between Greek *poleis* such as Thebes or Elis, where sexual unions between men and boys were promoted, and others where would-be pederasts were prohibited from even talking to boys. Spartan men were permitted to 'love' boys provided the man was of the 'right character', and his interest was 'innocent' out of 'admiration for a boy's personality'. This is why Xenophon explicitly connects 'men's love for boys' with their 'education'. Xenophon is frustratingly vague about what the boys learned from their lovers, but Plutarch suggests that the aim was to 'perfect the boy's character'. To illustrate this, Plutarch reveals that when a boy 'let slip a despicable cry' during a fight the ephors fined not him but his lover. Some modern scholars think that the 'inspirer' would also have smoothed his protégé's entry into his common mess when he became an adult.

While Xenophon sounds convincing about the asexual nature of Spartan pederasty, outsiders did not generally see it that way. Plato overtly rejected Sparta as a model for his ideal state—where pederasty was explicitly forbidden—because 'regarding passions of sex they contradict us', while the comic playwright Aristophanes regularly mocked the Spartans for their sexual interest in boys. Some ancient writers even suggested that the Spartans had a proclivity for anal intercourse with women too, with the term 'Laconian buttocks' (*kusolakôn*) becoming a popular euphemism for anal intercourse outside Sparta.

Some academics have attempted to explain Spartan pederasty by ethnographic comparison to warrior cultures where ritual homosexuality was practised in the context of pubertal initiations. In the light of practices amongst various Australasian tribal cultures whereby older males would engage in anal intercourse with younger initiates in the belief that the passing of semen would lead to physical growth and sexual maturity, some modern scholars have argued that the Spartans believed that the older mentor could pass on his masculine qualities to his young charge via his sperm. Some scholars have even taken a claim by Aelian (*c.*175–235 CE) that Spartan boys would ask their older inspirers to 'breathe into' them as indicating that the Spartans had practices similar to those documented amongst the Sambia of Papua New Guinea whereby pre-pubertal boys performed fellatio on sexually-mature youths in the belief that drinking their semen would make them courageous and strong. However, this conclusion distorts Aelian's testimony, for he clearly states that it was the older Spartan who was doing the 'breathing'.

There is, however, a possibility of having our cake and eating it too. In an obscure and fragmentary text, Cicero claims that regarding 'amatory relations' between young men, the Spartans 'allow them to embrace and to sleep together provided that they are separated by a cloak'. Modern experts have struggled to understand what Cicero means, but one intriguing suggestion (based partly on a

Laconian red-figure wine-cup from around 480 BCE depicting a couple engaging in intercrural sex while the *erômenos* is fully clothed) is that Spartans lovers were able to engage in full-on intercrural sex as long as their bodies were kept apart by a piece of clothing. If true, this would allow us to accept the testimony of Xenophon and Plutarch who claim that Spartans did not have sex with boys, and Aristophanes and Plato who insist they did.

Adult Education

Even after young Spartans joined a common mess and began fighting in the front line, older citizens continued to manage their behaviour. Xenophon says the Spartans showed the greatest concern for the *hêbôntes*, believing that these young adults would have the most influence for the good of the state if they had the right character. Plutarch puts it more bluntly: 'Spartiates' training extended into adulthood, for no one was permitted to live as he pleased'.

Young Spartan adults were probably not yet expected to marry, and at least some of them—if not all—slept in barracks in the city rather than in private homes. There is some scholarly debate as to whether young adults could yet grow their hair long, based partly on some garbled references in the sources as to what *hêbôntes* could and could not do to dress their hair. The confusion may simply originate in the fact that it takes some considerable time for anyone to grow their hair long after shaving their head. The *hêbôntes* also appear to have been denied the right to grow a moustache.

The behaviour of all the *hêbôntes* came under close scrutiny as they vied for a place in the elite Spartan infantry unit, the *hippeis* (literally 'knights', but recently translated by one scholar as 'knights-without-horses' to emphasize the fact that they fought on foot). The selection process for this group of 300 who served as a bodyguard for the king in battle was characteristically rigorous. The ephors selected three men who were called *hippagretai* ('knight-hunters'), who each chose a hundred *hêbôntes* to become the new *hippeis*. The *hippagretai* were required to justify their choices to the ephors, explaining both why they selected the men they did and why they rejected others. Plutarch tells us that when the *hippagretai* overlooked Pedaritus, who would later become an officer of some distinction in the fifth century BCE, he surprised his contemporaries by smiling broadly. When questioned why he looked so happy when he had been rejected, Pedaritus replied that he was smiling because he was delighted Sparta had 300 young men better than him! But not all Spartans took rejection so well. According to Xenophon the *hêbôntes* who missed out were on constant lookout for indiscretions by the *hippeis*, and the hostility between the two groups often led to violence, forcing older Spartiates to intervene. Any *hêbôntes* who refused to desist were hauled by the *paidonomos* before the ephors who levied a stiff fine to ensure that anger did not prevail over respect for law.

A final test some of the *hêbôntes* faced was the so-called *krypteia* ('secret-service'). Rather appropriately given its name, this institution whereby the smartest of the *hêbôntes* were sent out into the countryside armed only with a knife and carrying few provisions, is shrouded in mystery and contradiction. There are effectively two different traditions reflected in our sources: a 'hard' one reported by Aristotle, whereby the *kryptoi* ('the hidden') undergoing the *krypteia* were sent out with orders to hide by day and to slaughter any helots they encountered at night, and a 'soft' one preserved by Plato, who describes their task as 'a harsh form of training' in winter when young men 'wandered' with no footwear, bedding, or slaves to attend them.

Plutarch was so appalled by Aristotle's tale of *kryptoi* terrorizing the helot population that he refused to accept that an enlightened lawgiver like Lycurgus could have created such a 'foul exercise'. Instead, he argued that the helot-killing must have taken place only after the decade-long revolt by the helots in the 460s BCE. Some modern scholars have agreed, suggesting that a primitive initiation ritual whereby the youth was required to act as an 'anti-hoplite' before assuming full adult status and responsibilities morphed into a helot-terrorization operation over time. But it may be simply that the two traditions reflect outsiders' positive and negative attitudes to Sparta.

Only at age 30 could a Spartan truly consider himself one of the *homoioi*. With his training now complete he could sleep in his own home, and even grow a moustache. Yet even then Spartiates needed to ensure they did not tremble before the enemy in battle, or default on their contributions to their common mess. No adult Spartan, no matter how strong or wealthy, could ever truly feel sanguine about his status as one of the *homoioi*.

A School for Warriors?

Various explanations have been offered over the years as to the point of the Spartan upbringing. One option with a long tradition in modern scholarship is to take Xenophon at his word when he says that 'from the very beginning of childhood Spartans are trained and disciplined for land warfare'. Yet much of the upbringing, for example the singing, dancing, and athletics, was not directly related to warfare. Other modern scholars have compared the upbringing to 'primitive' rites of passage. But such cross-cultural studies tend to be highly selective, picking and choosing Spartan practices that fit with the thesis and overlooking the many Spartan practices that do not.

We also have to remember that the Spartan upbringing was not the fixed and unchanging entity that ancient writers such as Xenophon, Thucydides, and Plutarch believed it to be; it must have evolved over time. So it seems safest to follow the current orthodoxy which sees the upbringing as a set of comparatively typical 'maturation rituals' that trained the boys for their expected life as Spartan citizens, schooling them in Spartan values and ideals, and teaching them to overcome feelings or senses—the so-called *pathêmata*—such as fear (*phobos*), and shame/pride (*aidôs*), but also more physical feelings such as lust, hunger, and thirst. It will have also—as one recent study suggested—ensured that Spartiate children did not find playmates of inferior status such as helots or *perioikoi* and learn to identify with them instead of the older Spartiates!

Agesilaus is said to have described Spartan schooling as training in 'understanding how to take orders and give them'. Given that a Spartiate would have been required to spend much of his time either at war or anticipating being at war, the strong emphasis on obedience makes sense. Indeed, at the outbreak of the Peloponnesian War (431–404 BCE), the Spartan king Archidamus told the Spartiates that their strength lay in the fact that they obeyed orders with alacrity because they had been 'reared in the severest school'.

5

Spartan Women

Sparta's women were both famous and infamous in antiquity. Spartan women had a reputation for physical attractiveness which dated back to mythical times via Helen, whose beauty caused the decade-long Trojan War. But their beauty went hand in hand with a notoriety for sexual promiscuity, partly down to Helen's seduction by the Trojan prince Paris, but also because Spartan girls could be seen outside, scantily clad—allegedly even naked—and engaging in traditionally male activities like athletics. The Athenian playwright Euripides (c.480–406 BCE) wrote, 'No Spartan girl could ever be modest even if she wanted to be; they go outside their houses with the boys with naked thighs and open dresses and they race and wrestle with the boys. Insufferable!'. Furthermore, in a passage which excites interest disproportionate to its length, Plutarch even suggests that unmarried Spartan girls attracted the sort of 'love' from mature Spartan women that pubescent boys received from their 'inspirers'. No wonder then that outsiders like Aristotle (384–322 BCE), who condemned Sparta as a 'gynae-cocracy' (literally, 'power of/by women'), felt that Spartan women were out of control.

Loose Women?

The visual spectacle Spartan women provided was long-standing. The seventh-century BCE Spartan poet Alcman praised the beauty of numerous Spartan maidens, especially the lovely Hagesichora whose hair 'blooms like pure gold'. But unlike Hagesichora who clearly conformed to typical ancient world standards of decorum—Alcman praises her 'lovely ankles', a standard poetic epithet which reflects the fact that a modest or chaste girl was expected to be well covered—her Classical-period descendants were known as 'thigh-flashers' because of their short dresses. The Athenian tragedian Sophocles (497–405 BCE) described a Spartan girl as 'that young woman, whose tunic is unbelted around her thigh, revealingly', an image which matches numerous bronze figurines depicting muscular Spartan girls wearing short tunics with one breast exposed (Figure 12). These girls were not dressed so revealingly just to appeal to men; Spartan girls were famous for their athletic prowess in running, jumping, wrestling, throwing the discus and javelin, and dancing.

Aristophanes presents a striking image of Spartan womanhood in the character of Lampito (literally 'radiant') in his notorious play *Lysistrata* (411 BCE), in which the women of Greece compel their menfolk to end the Peloponnesian War (431–404 BCE) by organizing a Greece-wide sex strike. When Lampito strides onto stage her Athenian counterparts are stunned by her tanned and muscular physique, with Lysistrata remarking, 'Darling, what beauty you display! What a fine colour, and what a robust frame you've got! You could

Figure 12 Bronze figurine of Spartan girl running or dancing, c.520–500 BCE, British Museum.

throttle a bull!'; Lampito responds, 'Well, by the Twin gods, I think I could; at any rate I do gymnastics and jump heel to buttocks'. Lampito here is referring to the infamous Spartan 'rump jump' (*bibasis*), whereby girls would jump up and kick their own buttocks, first with one foot, then the other, followed by both at the same time. There were even competitions, with an epigram recording one Spartan girl's proud boast: 'I managed one thousand jumps in the *bibasis*, more than any other girl'. Lampito's size is no surprise given that Spartan women ate considerably better than other Greek women. In fact, one modern scholar has calculated that Spartan women could have consumed as much as 3,446 calories daily, considerably more than the 2,434 calories considered appropriate for a 'very active' female today.

Spartan girls did not exercise for the sake of it; it was part of their mandatory public training which bore some resemblance to that of the boys; indeed Plutarch (*c*.46–120 CE) says competing in traditionally male sports gave Spartan girls an air of 'masculine gallantry'. Whereas Spartan boys trained to prepare them for their future life as citizen-soldiers, Spartan girls were strengthening their bodies in preparation for their future role as child-bearers. There is no suggestion that Spartan girls were enrolled in 'herds' like the boys, and no source implies that they were ever required to sleep away from home.

On occasion Spartan girls would dance and sing naked in front of all the young men so that, as Plutarch puts it, they would be 'ashamed to be fat or weak'. No wonder then that one modern scholar recently suggested that participation in athletics reinforced norms that called for females to be compliant, beautiful objects of male desire. But the shaming culture could cut both ways, with Spartan girls singing songs praising the young men who were brave and strong, and mocking those who were weak or cowardly. One modern commentator notes that you can almost feel the boys' pain as they are being mocked by the naked teenage girls. My own feeling is that you can almost hear Plutarch's schoolboy giggling.

Although other Greeks saw Spartan female nudity as evidence of loose behaviour, Plutarch stresses that at Sparta it was 'altogether modest with no hint of immorality', and encouraged 'simple habits'—that is, no female finery. While this might seem rather hard to credit, it is worth bearing in mind that modern naturist communities see nothing sexual about their nudity.

Wordy Women

Spartan women were all the more notorious because they could be heard as well as seen. No fewer than forty sayings by Spartan women were recorded in antiquity, almost 10 per cent of all the preserved Spartan sayings. Perhaps the most famous and illuminating saying is one attributed to Leonidas' formidable wife Gorgo (whose name is rather appropriately derived from the mythical Gorgon whose fearsome visage turned men to stone); when asked by an Athenian woman why Spartan women were the only ones who could rule men, Gorgo replied, 'Because we are the only ones who give birth to men'. The majority of the sayings by Spartan women are motherly admonishments for failing to measure up to Spartan ideals. One particularly frightening Spartan mother reputedly hitched up her skirts and asked her cowardly son whether he wished to crawl back into her womb, while another bludgeoned her son to death with a roof tile for returning home alive when his comrades had fought to the death. Plutarch even records an epigram commemorating a Spartan mother who killed her son after learning he was a coward which reads: 'Damatrius was killed by his mother after breaking the law—she a Spartan lady, he a Spartan youth'. When one Spartan lad made the mistake of complaining to his mother that his sword was too short he suffered the blunt reply that he should just step closer to the enemy. Although many of these sayings are almost certainly fictional, they aptly demonstrate the fearsome reputation that Spartan women developed over time.

The wordiness of Spartan women stands in stark contrast to the rest of the Greek world—in particular Athens—where women were kept comparatively secluded. Sophocles wrote in his play *Ajax* that 'silence brings adornment to women', and a prominent and wealthy Athenian Ischomachus remarked to Socrates, 'I kept my wife under careful supervision so that she might hear and speak as little as possible' (sensationally after Ischomachus died his widow was seduced by her son-in-law). When the Athenian statesman Pericles could claim that a woman's greatest glory would be to be 'least talked of among men whether for good or bad' without censure it is no wonder that Spartan women caught the eye of admirers and critics alike.

Gorgo's saying that Spartan women ruled their men is matched by Plutarch's claim that Spartan men were 'always obedient to their wives'. It also matches Aristotle's complaint that Lycurgus 'entirely neglected' women, allowing them to live 'dissolutely in every respect' to the extent that Sparta became a gynaecocracy. Aristotle even suggested somewhat satirically that the Spartans could have overcome this excessive female influence if they had resorted more to peer-on-peer homosexuality! Given his claim elsewhere that 'silence is a woman's glory', it is not surprising that Aristotle was unimpressed by the forwardness of Spartan women. But we need to be careful when reading Aristotle, for Plutarch explicitly rejected his claims regarding Spartan women, arguing that Lycurgus actually 'showed all possible concern' for women. Sadly, Plutarch was not criticizing Aristotle out of an enlightened attitude to women; elsewhere he advised new husbands that 'a wife should speak only to her husband or through her husband'.

Wives and Mothers

Gorgo's famous claim that Spartan women were 'the only women who give birth to men' exposes the hard truth that for all their apparent liberation, the primary role of Spartan women was to give birth to the next generation of Spartiates. Xenophon contrasts Sparta with the rest of the Greek world where girls were expected 'to imitate the sedentary life that is typical of handicraftsmen—to keep quiet and do wool work', noting that Lycurgus decreed that slaves could make clothes, and that freeborn women should undertake physical training to prepare them for motherhood. Spartan girls also married later than their Athenian counterparts (who typically married close to puberty), the thought being that if girls married at their physical peak it would help in the production of 'sturdy' children. To help ensure that women were able to fulfil their child-bearing duties the Spartans even imposed a special law punishing mature-age bachelors, forcing them to parade naked around the market-place in the depths of winter, singing songs about how they were being justly punished. This may be the same festival at which Spartan women were said to have dragged unmarried men around a sacrificial altar while hitting them with sticks in order to make them fall in love and get married.

Plutarch reports that *hiereiai* (priestesses) were allowed grave markers like men who died in combat. Because Spartan memorial stones have been found bearing the words 'in childbirth', some modern scholars have advocated amending Plutarch's text to read 'women who died in childbirth' instead of priestesses. Some experts have even used this as evidence that death in childbirth when attempting to bear a new generation of Spartan warriors was the female equivalent of a 'beautiful death' in combat. But palaeographers insist that the original manuscript does not warrant such a change, and some academics question whether the Spartans would have treated women who had effectively failed in their duties as child-bearers with such distinction. My inclination is to follow those scholars who suggest that the term *hiereiai* at Sparta meant people of 'exceptional merit'—both Plato and Aristotle report that when the Spartans celebrated a good man they said he was 'god-like'—and that women who died in childbirth could fall into this category.

Ironically, Sparta's unusual sexual practices may have impeded Spartan women in their child-bearing role. We have already seen that Spartan husbands were discouraged from having sex with their wives too frequently, with the obvious negative implications for reproduction. But there were other peculiarities. Plutarch claims that the bride was 'carried off by force', and on her wedding day her head was shaved and she was forced to wear male clothing. Some modern scholars suggest their masculine appearance was intended to help inflame the passions of their young husbands who were used to male sexual partners. But one modern expert has suggested (rightly in my opinion) that the new bride's hair was cut off so that it lost its 'magic' quality that might entrance men. Xenophon reveals that it was shameful for a Spartan man to be seen entering or leaving his wife's sleeping quarters, so husbands had to sneak in at night when they desired sexual intercourse; anthropologists have noted similar practices amongst indigenous tribes in South America. Plutarch even claims that it was not uncommon for a wife to not see her husband in daylight for many years after their wedding. But that is surely hyperbole.

Helen's brothers Castor and Pollux (also known as either the Dioscuri or the 'Twin gods') provided a mythical precedent for this practice, having abducted the daughters of Leucippus who had been betrothed to the Messenian princes Idas and Lynceus, thus providing a mythical precedent for the hatred of the Spartans and Messenians too. We have one reliable historical example; Herodotus tells us that Leonidas' co-king Leotychides hated his cousin Demaratus because he had stolen Leotychides' betrothed, Percalus (whose name rather appropriately means 'very beautiful'), and literally carried her off. The notion that Leotychides was betrothed to Percalus seems to jar with the idea of abduction. But it may be Demaratus made an otherwise purely ritual abduction a reality. Another possibility is that Demaratus was able to assert a 'higher claim' by his seizing her first.

Hermippus of Smyrna (third century BCE) describes a bizarre Spartan form of speed-dating whereby unmarried girls were locked in a dark room with eligible young men, and each man married whichever girl he grabbed onto. Many modern experts dismiss this as a prime example of the kind of fairy tales other Greeks told about the Spartans. But some scholars have suggested that Hermippus' testimony might indicate there was one practice for the richer Spartans, like Leotychides and Demaratus, and another for poorer Spartans who struggled to find a spouse. Sayings by Spartan maidens that their dowry was the prized Spartan quality of 'self-control', or their father's good sense, indicate that poorer Spartan girls who lacked a dowry struggled to find a husband, as does another later source which claims that men who married undowried maidens were granted exemption from taxes. An alternative explanation for the groping in the dark ritual is that these bachelors were *mothakes* who were hoping for a leg-up in society, for Hermippus goes on to say that the Spartans fined Lysander (reportedly a *mothax*) for trying to swap the girl he grabbed in the dark for one who was more beautiful.

Spartan sexual practices were even more notorious owing to the fact that wife-sharing (*polyandry*) was apparently common amongst poorer Spartans. Xenophon tells us that if a man did not wish to be married but wanted to have children it was legal for him to have children by 'any fertile and well-bred woman', provided he had her husband's consent. Xenophon also reveals that if an older man had a young, fertile wife, he could 'introduce' her to a young man whose physical and moral qualities he admired for the purpose of begetting children. Polybius (*c.*200–118 BCE) even claims that it was 'common custom' for three or four Spartiates to share one wife. No wonder then that one Spartan when asked about the rules concerning adultery at Sparta replied, 'But how could there be an adulterer at Sparta?'

Wealthier Spartans practised endogamy (close-kin marriage), so much so that marriage between uterine half siblings was permitted, although marriage between siblings with the same father was illegal. We have too many examples of endogamy at Sparta for this to be an occasional thing. Most obvious is Leonidas' marriage to the daughter of his half-brother Cleomenes. Given the age gap between Leonidas and Gorgo, Leonidas was either widowed or divorced unbeknownst to us, or (perhaps more likely) Leonidas delayed marrying until Gorgo came of age so that the wealth of the two families could be combined. Anaxandridas, the father of Leonidas and Cleomenes, married his sister's daughter. We are told that when she failed to provide him with an heir the ephors insisted that Anaxandridas find a new wife, but he refused. A compromise was found whereby Anaxandridas committed legal bigamy. His new wife immediately fell pregnant with Cleomenes, but soon after his first wife fell pregnant too. The relatives of the new wife cried foul, so the ephors kept close watch when the first wife gave birth to Dorieus to ensure that no trickery took place. The fact that Anaxandridas bore no further children by his second wife, but fathered not only Dorieus but also Leonidas and Cleombrotus by his first wife, suggests there was genuine affection in their relationship. Nonetheless, Anaxandridas' refusal to divorce her was almost certainly partly motivated by a desire to keep her wealth within his family.

Depressingly for those who want to see Spartan women as feminist icons, their active and visible role seems to have diminished considerably after marriage. Although Aristophanes portrayed mature Spartan women like Lampito acting like young girls, it seems likely that their athletic activities ended once they were married. Heracleides Lembos (second century BCE) reveals that 'the world of Spartan women is deprived because they are not allowed to wear long hair, and cannot wear golden ornaments'. Mature Spartan women were even veiled like other Greek women. When asked why Spartan girls were unveiled but married women were, the Spartan king Charillus is said to have remarked, 'Because girls must find husbands, whereas married women must keep them'. Sadly this suggests that the everyday life of mature Spartan women might have been almost as restricted as that of their secluded Athenian counterparts.

Landholders and Landladies

One of the reasons that Aristotle could feel that Spartan women were permitted to act as they pleased was that, unlike most women throughout human history, they were able to own landed-property in their own right. Other Greek women only inherited land when they were the sole heir, and even then only as a token gesture until they married their nearest male relative (effectively a form of entailment). But Spartan daughters inherited property alongside their brothers, and it does not seem to have been the norm for the next of kin to marry sole heiresses. Rich mature Spartan widows may have been able to avoid remarriage altogether because of their greater financial independence. As Spartan citizen numbers declined in the later fifth century BCE the proportion of wealthy Spartan widows would have increased, which may have led to particularly female-dominated households, perhaps explaining why there are so many stories of Spartan boys being dominated by their mothers. Wealthy Spartan women would also have been able to provide financial assistance to poorer male relatives, which could have given some women even more influence over their men. The practice of polyandry would have given some Spartan women control of (or at least influence over) multiple households.

Some Spartan women were able to use their wealth and status to intrude on traditional male spheres, even competing against men at the Olympic Games in chariot racing, albeit by proxy as women were not able to compete in person. The owners of the horses did not need to be present to compete—thus Philip of Macedon was famously at home in Pella when he learned of his Olympic chariot victory in 356 BCE on the same day his son Alexander the Great was born. Agesilaus' sister Cynisca (literally, 'little bitch') won the blue riband event of the Olympics, the four-horse chariot race, *twice* in 396 and 392 BCE. Cynisca proudly set up a dedication at Olympia: 'My fathers and brothers were kings of Sparta. I, Cynisca, victorious with chariot of swift-footed horses, erected this statue. I declare that I am the only woman in all Greece to have taken the crown.' Cynisca was even accorded a sacred precinct close to the sanctuary of the divine Helen. Another Spartan woman, Euryleonis, is known to have been victorious in the Olympic two-horse chariot race in 368 BCE. For her achievement Euryleonis was awarded a statue on the acropolis, a typical way of celebrating male excellence.

Gynaecocracy?

As we have already seen, Aristotle thought Sparta was a gynaecocracy where women 'ruled' their men. This idea has caught the attention of many modern commentators, particularly feminist writers, who have sought to paint Sparta as some sort of feminist utopia. But the reality is not nearly so positive. A prime example is Cynisca's famous Olympic victory. Cynisca introduces herself to 'us' the reader via her male relatives, and, more depressingly, Xenophon says her brother Agesilaus encouraged her to compete because he had noticed that some Spartan men were taking great pride in breeding horses and wished to prove to them that 'this event was no proof of personal excellence, but merely the result of having some money and spending it'. So while Cynisca boasted of her equestrian achievements, her own brother allegedly denigrated them as an empty display of wealth.

Modern scholars also doubt the historicity of many of the sayings of Spartan women, which effectively takes away one of the main pillars supporting the notion of their power over men. In recent years scholars have been especially critical of one of the most iconic sayings—that of a mother exhorting her son to come back either carrying his shield or carried on it (literally she says 'with this, or on this', with appropriate Spartan brevity), a line which the film *300* gives to Gorgo when she says farewell to Leonidas. This saying essentially means that the Spartiate should return home from battle still bearing his shield (as dropping one's shield was a sign of cowardice throughout Greece), or return from battle carried on it, that is, as a dead man. But modern experts frequently deny the historicity of this saying because Spartans who fell in battle were not brought home for burial, but instead interred in the *polyandrion* at the battle site. However, it may be that scholars who reject this saying are being too literal in their interpretation. Xenophon tells us that there was a group of Spartan soldiers called 'shield bearers' who carried the wounded and dead from the field of battle back to the camp using shields as stretchers. So this famous saying might be rescued by understanding it as meaning 'return *to camp* with this or on this'.

When it came to warfare, despite their famed physical training, Spartan women were even less helpful than their secluded counterparts in other Greek *poleis*. Other Greek women did on occasion play a useful role in fighting, 'manning' city walls during sieges and showering besiegers with stones and broken roof tiles. The Spartans were even said to have been thwarted in their efforts to capture the city of

Argos *c.*494 BCE by the bravery of the Argive women led by the poetess Telesilla. But the absence of city walls at Sparta denied Spartan women this traditional female role in fighting. When Sparta was invaded by the Thebans in 362 BCE it was Sparta's boys and old men who showered the enemy with missiles, not the women. Aristotle explicitly criticizes the Spartan women for their failure to help, and argues that the commotion the panicking women generated actively hindered the Spartiates. But it seems likely that the Spartans consciously denied women the opportunity to help because their primary role was that of bearing the next generation of Spartans. Spartan men could risk their lives in battle, but women needed to be kept safe to bear more children to replace those who made the ultimate sacrifice for Sparta. It has also been suggested that Aristotle may have been mistaken, and that the Spartan women were raucous not because they were afraid, but because they were frustrated at being denied the opportunity to help. Nearly a century later, when Pyrrhus of Epirus invaded Sparta, Sparta's maidens and matrons insisted on helping; they joined the old men digging a defensive ditch around the city, some hitching up their long robes around their waists, and others wearing only under-tunics.

One modern expert recently suggested that it was not so much that Spartan women ruled their men, but rather that they 'judged' them, offering both 'the emollient of praise and the sting of abuse'. This in itself allowed Spartan women quite a degree of influence, with the awarding or withholding of praise offering them a form of social control. Sparta was no gynaecocracy, but Spartan women certainly left their mark.

6

Helots

It is difficult to overstate the importance of the helots to the Spartan way of life. Put simply, exploiting helot labour in Laconia and Messenia allowed the Spartans to become what modern scholars call 'absentee landlords', freeing them to pursue their Spartiate gentlemanly lifestyle. This is why the Athenian admirer of Sparta, Critias (c.460–403 BCE), regarded Sparta as the place where one could find men who were 'most free' and 'most unfree'—that is, the Spartiates and the helots. Despite the helots' importance to Spartan society we actually know comparatively little about them. Indeed, one recent modern study noted (somewhat hyperbolically) helots have been so thoroughly effaced from history that not one helot name or even one word spoken by a helot has been preserved.

Plato (c.428–347 BCE) wrote that 'the helot system of Sparta is practically the most discussed and controversial subject in Greece, some approving the institution, others criticizing it'. Helotry is still probably the most discussed and controversial topic regarding Sparta. But today's controversy is not whether helotry should be admired or criticized, but rather the nature of the relationship between the

Spartans and the helots they exploited. Were the helots a resentful 'human volcano' ready to erupt as one modern Marxist scholar suggested? Or did the helots show a 'considerable measure of acquiescence' as one revisionist suggests?

Much of the modern debate centres on the seemingly definitive observation by Thucydides (*c.*460–400 BCE) that 'Spartan policy has always been determined by the necessity of taking precautions against the helots'. This statement has led some commentators to see Spartan history as fundamentally shaped by 'class struggle' between the Spartans and the helots, with the whole Spartan way of life designed to counter the 'helot threat'. This line of thought sees the acquisition of Messenia as a double-edged sword for the Spartans, who can be likened to Fafnir from Norse myth, who transformed himself into a dragon to safeguard his hoard of stolen gold and was consequently unable to enjoy it.

But the latest scholarship suggests that the Spartans only really developed their distinctive lifestyle several generations after the conquest of Messenia, which completely undermines the Fafniresque image of Spartan society. Moreover, Thucydides' crucial sentence can also be translated as 'most Spartan relations with helots were precautionary in character', which permits a less hostile interpretation of Spartan–helot relations. No one would suggest that there was no hostility between the Spartans and helots. But the sheer size of the Spartan state, and the fact that the Spartans were mostly obliged to remain in the town of Sparta itself, has rightly led some modern scholars to question why we have such little evidence of helots actively rebelling against their masters if relations were so hostile. As one of my recent students eloquently phrased it, the helot volcano seems mostly dormant. Nonetheless, no one can deny that the Spartans often horribly mistreated the helots. It is a theme that will recur throughout this chapter.

Agricultural Labourers

Helots were primarily agricultural labourers for their Spartiate masters, supplying the barley, wine, olive oil, cheese, and pork that they required for membership of the common messes. As Aristotle (384–322 BCE) bluntly put it, 'it is the helots who farm the land for the benefit of the Spartiates'. This explains a saying attributed to Cleomenes, that whereas Homer, who told the stories of the warrior heroes Achilles, Ajax, Odysseus, and Hector, was 'the poet of the Spartiates', Hesiod, who wrote a didactic poem about everyday life and agriculture called *Works and Days*, was 'the poet of the helots'.

Some of our sources claim that the helots were required to hand over a 'fixed payment' (*apophora*) from the produce of the lands they tilled, but others suggest it was a proportion (*moira*), that is 'share-cropping'. The difference between 'portion' and 'proportion' is not merely semantic. A fixed rent, for example the 82 *medimnoi* (around 3,000 kg) of barley Plutarch (*c*.46–120 CE) says Spartiates were required to contribute to the messes would have been more practical to manage because the Spartiate landowner would not need to worry about his helots concealing produce, or need to incentivize his helots to produce enough to cover his needs. Furthermore, in years of poor yield, a fixed amount would have been potentially disastrous for helots because their Spartiate masters would surely have attended to their own needs first given their citizen status depended on that fixed amount. One need only think of the catastrophic Irish potato famine in the 1840s when the failure of the potato crop caused around a million Irish tenants to die of starvation and another million to emigrate, while their English and Anglo-Irish landlords exported other food produce from their estates for profit.

If the amount required was a proportion, for example the 50 per cent indicated by Tyrtaeus (seventh century BCE), in lean years both the helots and their masters would suffer. But provided enough produce was harvested for helot workers to survive, the consequences of serious crop failures under such a system could have been more devastating for the Spartiate master than the helot. For whereas the helot workers could scrape by for a year, the landowner might default on his mess contribution and be reduced to 'inferior' status. For this reason it seems more likely that the Spartiates would have required the helots to hand over *at least* the amount they required for their mess contributions.

It is important to consider how many helots there would have been, because their numerical strength effectively conditioned the population size and prosperity of the Spartiates. Over the years modern estimates of the numbers of helots have ranged from 375,000 to 140,000, with the helots outnumbering the Spartiates from 7:1 to as much as 20:1. But most of these figures are little more than speculation, because no surviving source provides even a rough estimate for the number of helots. However, in recent years, some scholars have attempted to determine how many citizens and helots the arable land available to the Spartiates could have supported by exploiting data from modern Greek censuses, archaeological surveys of land usage in Laconia and Messenia, and the latest research on ancient Mediterranean agrarian practices. There is by no means a scholarly consensus about this sort of quantitative analysis, but stepping back from the differences in methodology and conclusions, these studies suggest that the Spartiates would have owned 115,000–145,000 hectares of arable land, with a mean Spartiate landholding size of around 20 hectares, albeit not necessarily in one discrete parcel. Although such landholdings would be considerably larger than the typical ancient Greek family farm, modelling suggests that the Spartiates' holdings would have supported a much smaller helot population than previously thought, somewhere in the range of 75,000–120,000, with perhaps only 35,000–55,000 adult male helots.

It is unclear how Spartiate estates were managed. Modern scholars agree that it would have been comparatively easy for Spartiates to inspect their estates in Laconia which were largely located close to the cluster of villages that made up the 'city' of Sparta. But their estates in Messenia, which were separated from Sparta by the long Taygetus mountain range (2,404 metres at the peak), could not have been easily or regularly inspected. As their citizen status depended on the effective management of these often far-flung estates, most modern scholars assume the Spartiates kept managers in place to oversee their helots. Hesychius of Alexandria (fifth or sixth century CE) records the terms '*mnoionomoi*, leaders of helots', and '*mnoia*, group of slaves', which seems to prove this theory. Most modern experts assume that Hesychius' 'helot leaders' were helots themselves, locals who engaged in what has been called 'privileged collaboration' with their masters to ensure the smooth running of Spartiate estates. A potentially useful comparative is the fact that in *ante-bellum* South Carolina some absentee white slave owners used slave 'drivers' to oversee the activities of their fellow slaves, rather than paying free white overseers. Other experts suggest that the Spartiates would have employed outsiders, perhaps from the nearby communities of *perioikoi*, to oversee their estates.

Other Helot Duties

Some helots performed domestic tasks that elsewhere would have been carried out by chattel slaves or even poor free women. Thus, we hear of helot men serving as household stewards, and helot women acting as wet-nurses for children, making clothes (a task which elsewhere in Greece would have often been performed by wives and unmarried daughters), and even serving as ladies-in-waiting to Spartan queens.

The Spartans also made considerable use of helots in warfare. We have already seen that helots were present with Leonidas and his 300 at Thermopylae, and Herodotus (*c.*484–425 BCE) reports that the Spartans took 35,000 helots to fight alongside them at the Battle of Plataea the following summer. These helots were not mere attendants like those at Thermopylae; Herodotus explicitly states that they were 'equipped for war'. Some must have died in the fighting, for Herodotus tells us the Spartans set up separate monuments for their dead, two for themselves and another one for the helots.

The use of helots as soldiers suggests a certain degree of trust in them on the part of the Spartiates. But it definitely should not be seen as evidence that the Spartans were sanguine about helot loyalty. Critias wrote that the Spartans so mistrusted the helots that when the Spartans were at home they removed the arm-strap (*porpax*) from their shields to prevent the helots from using their shields against them. Critias adds that because it was impractical to remove the *porpax* on campaign Spartiates always kept their spears in hand, just in case the helots should seize their shields and 'attempt an uprising'. Although Xenophon (*c.*430–354 BCE) does not mention the helots in this context, fear of their potential for trouble could help explain why the Spartans rather oddly set up their military camps in a circle, facing inwards, rather than outwards towards the enemy.

Slaves or Serfs?

There is considerable confusion about the helots' actual status. Helots did the work of slaves, but they were not normally referred to as *douloi*, the generic Greek term for slaves. Nonetheless, the so-called Peace of Nicias between Sparta and Athens (421 BCE) included a clause 'should the slave population (*douleia*) rise, the Athenians shall help the Lacedaemonians with all their might', and

Xenophon lumps the helots together with horses and hunting dogs, types of *tetrapoda* ('four-footed things'), which suggests that he perceived helots as other Greeks saw chattel slaves, that is as *andrapoda* 'man-footed things'.

Their name 'helots'—actually *heilôtai*—might derive from the Greek verb *haliskomai* which means 'to take', or it might have the same Indo-European root as the Old Norse 'seil' which meant 'rope' or 'bond', thus making the helots 'bondsmen'. Both possibilities fit well with the tradition that the helots were originally prisoners of war. We can safely discount the ancient claim that the helots were called so after the Laconian community Helos which rebelled unsuccessfully against Sparta in the eighth century BCE, for Helos would need to be Heilos with an ei diphthong for this to be true.

Some sources refer to helots as 'public slaves' (*dêmosioi*), and Strabo (64 BCE–*c*.24 CE) claims that it was illegal to liberate helots or sell them outside the boundaries of Sparta. This has prompted some modern experts to argue the helots were owned by the Spartan state rather than their Spartiate masters. Other sources claim the helots had a status 'between freemen and slaves', which leads some historians to argue that helots were 'serfs' like those in early modern Russia, who could be moved between estates, converted to domestic duties, or bought and sold.

The confusion about the status of helots is not helped by the fact that it is unclear whether Spartans also owned regular chattel slaves for domestic duties. Some sources refer to household servants at Sparta using generic terms for household slaves like *oiketês*, but other times they specify that the servants are helots. For example, Herodotus tells us that

Ariston was told of the birth of his son Demaratus by 'one of his household' which could mean a regular slave, a helot playing that role, or technically even a free person, but explicitly tells us that the 'household member' who guarded the deranged Cleomenes was a helot. But the distinction may be unnecessary. Arrian (*c*.86–160 CE) claims that no one is technically a *doulos* at Sparta because 'the helots are the *douloi* among the Lacedaemonians and do the work of *douloi*', so it is possible that the helots were just the Spartan version of chattel slaves. Indeed one recent study of Greek slavery suggests that the term 'helotic slavery' could be applied as a 'rubric' to cover similar slave practices elsewhere in the Greek world.

Mass Conquest?

As noted earlier, there was a tradition dating back to Tyrtaeus in the seventh century BCE that the helots were the original inhabitants of Laconia and Messenia who had been defeated and enslaved by the Spartans. Later sources saw no reason to doubt this story. Theopompus (*c*.380–*c*.315 BCE) says, 'The race of the helots is in a completely savage and harsh state, for they have been enslaved by the Spartiates for a very long time'. The helots' status as a conquered nation can also be seen in Aristotle's testimony that the ephors declared war on them each year so that Spartans could kill them without incurring the religious pollution ancient Greeks believed came from an unlawful killing.

Unfortunately our only narrative sources for the Spartan conquest of Messenia post-date the liberation of the

Messenian helots in 370 BCE. The newly-freed Messenians needed a back story, and the result was a myth-history that cast the helots as a long-suffering conquered nation who ultimately triumphed over their heartless and abusive masters. But most of these stories are dubious, and many modern experts question whether it was even possible in antiquity for one nation to conquer and enslave another nation as the Spartans are said to have done with the Messenians. Several scholars argue that such a mass enslavement would be unparalleled in human history. But, as awful as it sounds, the Spartan enslavement of the Messenians was not believed to be unparalleled even in ancient Greece. The agricultural labourers in Thessaly in central Greece known as the *penestae* (derived from the verb 'to toil') were also said to be aboriginal peoples conquered by later incomers, and the Peloponnesian Greeks from Megara who set up the colony of Heracleia Pontica on the Black Sea reputedly conquered and enslaved the local Mariandynians, agreeing not to sell them beyond the boundaries of their homeland.

Ultimately my sympathies lie with modern scholars who believe that the Spartans really did conquer Messenia, but that the conquest was far more gradual than our sources imply. It may be that the argument here is too much about the semantics of the term 'conquest'. Yes, it seems difficult—if not impossible—for the ancient Spartans to have conquered and enslaved the *whole population* of Messenia. But, sadly, it does not seem difficult to imagine that they defeated and enslaved *some* of the Messenians, particularly if they did so in stages. It may be that the Messenian helots were captive peasant labourers, and that the Spartans simply supplanted an existing Messenian elite who had been exploiting peasants just as the Spartans themselves were already making use of servile labour in Laconia. Another appealing suggestion is that the 'conquest' of Messenia was essentially one long act of extortion, with the Spartiates making an 'annual demand for booty'—that is, 50 per cent of the produce of the land—which they shared amongst themselves, just as the mythical Greek heroes like Achilles, Odysseus, and Agamemnon shared the spoils of war when fighting the Trojans.

It is worth bearing in mind that half a century after they took control of Messenia the Spartans are said to have tried to enslave their northern neighbours the Tegeans too. Herodotus tells us that the pious Spartans asked Apollo whether they could conquer the whole of Arcadia (around $3,000\,km^2$). Apollo declined, but promised that they would 'beat their feet' on the 'beautiful plains' of Tegea and measure them with a rope. Upon hearing this the Spartans marched confidently into battle carrying iron fetters to chain up the vanquished Tegeans, which has prompted some modern scholars to speculate that this was not so much a land grab, but an attempt to acquire more slave labour. But oracles could be ambiguous; the Spartans ended up losing the so-called 'Battle of the Fetters', and many of them ended up temporarily beating Tegean fields with their feet not in dance, but as agricultural labourers in a chain gang, bound by their own fetters! Herodotus reports that he saw the Spartans' fetters, which the Tegeans dedicated to the goddess Athena Alea, when he visited Tegea more than a century later. The fetters could still be seen when Pausanias visited Athena's temple 600 years later. Although the Spartans were unsuccessful in their attempt to enslave the Tegeans, the fact that they even tried suggests they believed the conquest of Messenia could be repeated.

Spartan Brutality

Plutarch calls the Spartans' treatment of the helots 'callous and brutal'. Sometimes helots were forced to drink large quantities of unmixed wine and brought into the common messes to show Spartan young men what drunkenness was like. On other occasions helots were forced to perform ridiculous songs and dances that pointedly contrasted with the dignified choral performances of their masters. Myron of Priene (third century BCE) reports that helots were given a stipulated number of beatings regardless of whether they had done anything wrong, and were forced to wear a dog-skin cap and a leather jerkin (*diphthera*). Modern scholars sometimes interpret the Spartans as 'animalizing' the helots with these uniforms. This perhaps makes sense for the dog-skin cap, but the *diphthera* was a garment typically worn by poor labourers throughout the Greek world.

Critias notes that 'the Spartans permit themselves the authority to murder helots', which is almost certainly a reference to the ephors' annual declaration of war which Aristotle mentions. Aristotle also claims that young Sparti-ates participating in the *krypteia* made their way through the fields, 'killing all the helots who stood out for their physique and strength', and murdered any helots they found on the roads at night. This seems to match Myron's testimony that the Spartans put to death any helot who appeared 'robust beyond that which was fitting for a slave', and even fined their masters, for 'not having cut short their vigorous growth'. The Spartans' readiness to kill helots stands in stark contrast to the caution they showed when executing their own kind, with Thucydides claiming the Spartans were usually careful not to take 'irremediable steps' against Spartiates.

These killings must have terrorized the helot population. But nothing could have terrorized the helots more than a story Thucydides tells of the Spartans secretly massacring 2,000 helots after promising freedom to those who had most distinguished themselves in war. The 'lucky' helots who were chosen by their fellow helots donned garlands and went around the temples celebrating their emancipation. But what none of the helots knew was that this was a test, with the Spartans thinking that those selected would be the most 'high-spirited' and therefore the most likely to rebel. The Spartans murdered all 2,000, and although Plutarch implies that the massacre was perpetrated by the *krypteia*, Thucydides claims no one ever knew how they perished.

But this story of cold-blooded brutality is controversial. Some academics doubt that the Spartans could have secretly massacred so many men without access to modern technology, although the *Kaiadas* crevasse would be an obvious means of eliminating thousands of helots in a hurry. Other commentators argue that Thucydides might have been duped by either the Spartans who wanted outsiders to think this was the kind of thing they did, or escaped Messenian helots who wanted to darken the Spartans' reputation. Another possibility is that the Spartans really did intend to reward the helots but changed their mind after so many bold and therefore potentially dangerous helots volunteered. Nearly a century later when the Thebans invaded Sparta they offered freedom to helots who would fight on their behalf, but panicked when more than 6,000 accepted the call. Whatever the reality might be, the story certainly reflects the complex relationship between the Spartans and the helots.

Perhaps the most revealing story about the treatment of helots is one told by Plutarch in the context of the liberation of Messenia by the Thebans. When the Thebans insisted that some captive helots could now sing songs by Terpander, Alcman, and Spendon—that is, the songs that the Spartiates would normally sing—the helots declined on the grounds that their masters would not approve. Their refusal is interpreted by modern scholars as a sign of either 'Stockholm syndrome' style loyalty to their masters or abject fear of them. Either way it shows the immense psychological pressure the Spartans placed on the helots.

Rebels with a Cause

Although modern scholars debate the extent to which the helots offered a threat to their Spartiate masters, it is undeniable that on occasions their resentment bubbled over into active revolt. We have already seen that the elegies Tyrtaeus wrote were intended to inspire the Spartans to overcome the Messenians who rebelled in the mid-seventh century BCE. Tyrtaeus speaks of the Spartans having tasted both victory and defeat, and it seems to me that his description of the defeated as labouring 'like asses exhausted under great loads' is intended to evoke not pity for the defeated rebels, but a sense of *Schadenfreude* at the suffering of a hated foe. Plato complains that the helots betrayed the Greeks by rebelling in 490 BCE and preventing the Spartans from helping the Athenians at the Battle of Marathon, although many modern commentators doubt this claim. The helot 'human volcano' erupted spectacularly in 464 BCE, when an earthquake that rocked Sparta sparked a ten-year rebellion that shook Spartan society to the core. Finally, in 370 BCE the helots in Messenia successfully rebelled with Theban assistance, and formed a new *polis* of their own.

By all accounts the earthquake that struck Laconia in 464 BCE and the subsequent helot rebellion were shattering events for the Spartans. Diodorus (writing 60–30 BCE) claims that 20,000 Lacedaemonians were killed in the earthquake and the aftershocks that followed (if true, this figure must include women, children, and *perioikoi*) and Plutarch tells us that all the Spartan youths were killed when the gymnasium collapsed—their tomb, the Seismatias ('the shaking'), could still be seen in his day—and that the city of Sparta was demolished with the exception of five houses. Some modern scholars have speculated that Thucydides' notorious statement about Sparta's lack of architectural grandeur may reflect his visit to a city that never really recovered from the earthquake.

The helots seized their opportunity and revolted *en masse*, as did two perioikic towns. We are told that only the swift actions of King Archidamus who seized his armour and called on the Spartiates to follow his example saved the city from the hordes of helots who had gathered from around the countryside aiming to dispatch the surviving Spartiates. The revolt in Laconia appears to have been put down swiftly; Diodorus says that the helots abandoned any hope of capturing the city of Sparta when they saw that Archidamus had put together an army, and they withdrew to their communities. But the revolt in Messenia was no small incident. Herodotus tells us that Arimnestus, who had slain Xerxes' nephew Mardonius at the Battle of Plataea in 479 BCE, led 300 Spartans to battle at Stenyclerus against 'the whole army of Messenia', and was killed along with all his men. But ultimately the rebels were forced to dig in at a stronghold on Mt Ithome. The Spartans were unable to dislodge them and called on outsiders for help. Somewhat surprisingly this call-out included their great rival Athens. Although the leading democratic Athenian leaders agitated against it, Cimon, a conservative politician who was so pro-Spartan he named his eldest son Lacedaemonius ('Spartan'), persuaded the Athenians not to abandon their former 'yoke-partner' during the war against Xerxes.

But the Spartans did not reward the Athenians for their assistance; instead they singled them out amongst all the allies and demanded they leave. Although the Spartans did not state why the Athenians were no longer required, Thucydides says the Athenians felt that the Spartans feared that the Athenians might be tempted to side with the helots against them. Some modern scholars have speculated that the Spartans thought that the democratic Athenians might sympathize with the plight of the Messenian manual labourers more than they did with the wealthy Spartans, especially once they learned that the helots spoke Greek and were not foreign 'barbarians' like their own slaves. This incident destroyed any lingering friendship between the Athenians and Spartans that still existed from the war against Xerxes, and made the later war between them (the Peloponnesian War 431–404 BCE) almost inevitable. The siege of the rebels on Mt Ithome dragged on for ten years. The truce which ended it stipulated that the rebels would leave the Peloponnese and never return, and that if any helot returned he would automatically become the slave (*doulos*) of his captor—food for thought for anyone who doubts that the helots were real 'slaves'. The Athenians set up the evacuees in the city of Naupactus in central Greece, showing favour to the Messenians just as the Spartans had feared.

This rebellion appears to have been a defining moment in Spartiate–helot relations, and later it came to be seen as a full-blown nationalist uprising by the Messenians. Plutarch suggests that it was only after the rebellion that such harsh practices as the *krypteia* took place, and some modern scholars argue that it was only then that the ephors' annual declaration of war on the helots came into being. If so, rather ironically, the Spartans' attempts to control the helots might have sowed the seeds of their own destruction, by helping to foster not only an adversarial mindset but also a collective Messenian identity.

Half a century later in 370 BCE, when the Thebans invaded Lakônikê with a massive army following their victory over the Spartans at Leuctra, the Messenians rose up one final time, and this time they were able to make it count. The Theban general Epaminondas gathered together the inhabitants of Messenia, divided the land amongst them, and founded a city for them, allegedly doing all this in just eighty-five days. The foundation of the new Messenian *polis* was the death-knell for Spartan power, partly because so very many Spartiates were financially crippled by the loss of their estates in Messenia that the entire fabric of the Spartan social order unravelled. Aristotle later wrote that the Spartan state was defective because it did not withstand 'a single blow'; it is not entirely clear whether he meant the defeat at Leuctra or the loss of Messenia, or both. But together these blows really did end Sparta's greatness. The new Messenian *polis* proved to be such a thorn in Sparta's side that one modern scholar has described the Messenian helots as 'long-term losers who ultimately triumph'. But we should spare a thought for the Laconian helots for whom there was no such happy ending; they remained under Sparta's brutal rule for many generations to come.

7

The Later Reception of Sparta

This final chapter focuses on the 'reception' of Sparta in modern culture, by which I mean the ways in which the ancient testimony about the Spartans has been transmitted, interpreted, represented, and reimagined by later societies. The modern history of ancient Sparta is almost as fascinating as the ancient history is, and no short treatment could hope to be comprehensive. My aim here is to provide a snapshot of the enduring legacy of the Spartans in more recent history and culture.

Famous Opinions on Sparta—the Good, the Bad, and the Ugly

Almost anyone who was anyone over the last two millennia has had an opinion on the Spartans, both good and bad. The Spartans even make an appearance in the Catholic and Orthodox version of the Old Testament, in *Maccabees*, where it is revealed the third-century BCE Spartan king Areus wrote to Onias, the high priest at Jerusalem, to convey the startling news that 'the Spartans and Jews are brothers and are of the family of Abraham'. Although the Romanized Jewish historian Flavius Josephus (37–100) also claimed this happened, the story is usually dismissed by modern scholars as a fabrication by Jonathan, the second-century BCE high priest, who was seeking a military alliance with Sparta against the Seleucids. Josephus' contemporary, the otherwise philhellenic Roman emperor Nero (37–68), allegedly refused to travel to Sparta because its austerity jarred with his extravagant lifestyle, whereas Trajan (53–117) exploited Sparta's legendary past for his own ends by reinstating the Leonidas festival at Sparta when he was about to wage his own West vs East war against the Parthians. The pagan emperor Julian 'the Apostate' (331–63) rather oddly insisted that Lycurgus was a superior legislator to Moses because he was less cruel. Sparta's legendary status can been seen in the fact that St. Gregory, Bishop of Tours (c.538–94), felt the need to invent a Spartan king with the very Roman name Festus to be a contemporary to King Solomon.

In the Middle Ages Martin Luther (1483–1546) noted the toughness of Spartan 'ironmen'. Machiavelli (1469–1527) was 'firmly convinced' that the way to set up a long-lasting republic was to constitute it like Sparta. Many Enlightenment-period thinkers stressed their admiration for the Spartans and their way of life. Jean-Jacques Rousseau (1712–78) said of Sparta: 'one saw the rise of this city, as renowned for its happy ignorance as for the wisdom of its Laws, this Republic of demigods rather than men', while his rival Gabriel Bonnot de Mably (1709–85) described himself as 'an austere Spartophile lost in the streets of Paris'. The painter Jacques-Louis David (1748–1825) devoted literally years of his life (1799–1803 and 1813–14) to producing his colossal work *Leonidas at Thermopylae*, which depicts a naked Leonidas at its centre, his eyes turned toward the heavens, suggesting he knows his fate. On the left, a Spartan soldier carves the famous 'Go tell the Spartans' epigram on a cliff face, while other naked and semi-nude soldiers embrace or don their armour in preparation for their final stand.

But other Enlightenment-era commentators were less convinced by the Spartans. Voltaire (1694–1778) asked aggressively, 'What good did Sparta do for Greece?', Denis Diderot (1713–84) dismissed them as 'monks bearing arms', and when Napoleon (1769–1821) saw David's painting he asked why he had bothered to paint the defeated. Many of the Founding Fathers of the USA were also critical of Sparta, including Thomas Jefferson (1743–1826) who dismissed the Spartans as 'military monks' ruling over helots 'reduced to abject slavery', and Alexander Hamilton (1755–1804), who wrote disparagingly, 'Sparta was little better than a well-regulated camp'.

The English poet and politician Richard Glover (1712–85) was moved to write an epic poem entitled *Leonidas* (1737) in nine books. Glover's work begins with the Homeric lines, 'Rehearse, O Muse, the deeds and glorious death, Of that fam'd Spartan, who withstood the pow'r Of Xerxes near Thermopylae, and fell To save his country'. It was very popular in its day, and was translated into German four times. Lord Byron (1788–1824) was a committed Spartophile despite having been born disabled. In his *Don Juan*

(1819) Byron asked for just three proper Spartans to help liberate Greece from the Ottoman Turks: 'Earth! render back from out thy breast A remnant of our Spartan dead! Of the three hundred grant but three. To make a new Thermopylae!' This was not idle talk on Byron's part, as the poet travelled to Greece to fight in the Greek War of Independence (although he succumbed to fever before seeing any real action).

Although he was repelled by the warlike brutality of the Spartans, the German philosopher Friedrich Nietzsche (1844–1900) admired their 'Dorian' physical conditioning. In German-speaking circles the terms 'Dorian' and 'Spartan' later came to be synonymous with racial purity, with Social-Darwinists such as Ernst Haeckel (1834–1919) speaking of 'Spartan selection' in the same breath as 'natural selection'. This line of thought heavily influenced Adolf Hitler (1889–1945) who in 1928 praised the Spartans' exposure of sick, weak, and deformed children as 'the best example of the racial policy'. Spartan-style displays of courage also appealed to Hitler, who in April 1945 told Martin Bormann 'A desperate fight will always be remembered as a worthy example . . . just think of Leonidas and his 300 Spartans'. Hermann Göring (1893–1946) was also an ardent admirer of Leonidas. During the last days of the Battle of Stalingrad in 1943 he invoked the 'Go tell the Spartans' epigram, telling German troops from the Sixth Army: 'If you go to Germany, tell them you have seen us fighting in Stalingrad, obedient to the law'. Ironically the Soviet troops at Stalingrad also compared themselves to Leonidas and the Spartans. But there was a limit to Nazi Spartophilia: both Göring and Hitler rejected a proposed suicide squadron for the Luftwaffe using a manned version of the V-I flying bomb—the so-called 'the Leonidas Staffel'—on the grounds that such self-sacrifice was not in keeping with the German character.

In March 1976 the soon-to-be US president Ronald Reagan (1911–2004) complained that Henry Kissinger (1923–) 'thinks of the United States as Athens and the Soviet Union as Sparta', dismissing Kissinger's fears that 'effete' Athens would be defeated by 'vigorous and disciplined' Sparta. More recently Leonidas' famous saying '*molôn labe*' has been used as an unofficial slogan by the National Rifle Association and other North American firearm enthusiasts in their vigorous campaign against gun control. Such is the Spartans' modern reputation for military toughness, gamers playing the highly-successful first-person shooter video game franchise *Halo* control super-soldiers codenamed 'Spartans'.

We have already seen the impact Sparta had on the modern English language via the adjectives 'spartan' and 'laconic'. But other Spartan terms crossed over into English too. Eighteenth-century Irish peasants were referred to disparagingly as 'helots' by English writers, and it is even possible that the word 'oik', which was first used as school slang for uneducated 'provincial' types in the nineteenth century, derives from the adaption of *perioikoi* by wealthy boys at English fee-paying public schools to describe the locals who lived around them! This makes sense given that many of the leading English and Scottish fee-paying schools implicitly appropriated Spartan values in their day-to-day practice in the nineteenth century, and some, such as Loretto in Scotland, adopted the Latin motto—borrowed from Cicero—*Spartam nactus es, hanc exorna* (Sparta is yours, adorn it).

The Spartans also had an impact on the German language, with students at Prussian cadet schools in the nineteenth century coining the verb 'spartanern' for heroic resistance to pain, and prizing the quality of *Spartanertum* ('Spartanness'). This can be seen in the 1898 children's novel *Spartanerjünglinge: Eine Kadettengeschichte in Briefen* (*The Spartan Youth: A Cadet Story in Letters*). Set in the years 1867–8, the book charts the life and death of a Royal Prussian Cadet, Gerhard von Gottwein. As the title suggests, the Spartans are never far from the action, with Gerhard writing to his mother about how in their history lessons the cadets 'learn all about' the Spartan boy 'hero' who stole the fox cub, and how they emulate his exploits with a Spartan-style code to never weep or tell tales. Gerhard dies showing true *Spartanertum*, refusing to inform on the bullying cadet who brought on his fatal bout of pneumonia by trapping him in a freezing locker room.

Sparta has even had an impact on the modern landscape, with scores of communities and literally hundreds of roads across North America named Sparta, Spartanburg, or even Spartansburg, after *the* Sparta, speaking volumes for American admiration for the Spartans. There is even a 'Spartan' apple, developed by a formal scientific breeding programme in British Columbia in 1936, which rather appropriately has a bright-red blush.

The Darker Side of Spartan Reception

The later history of ancient Sparta is often a troubled one, owing to a combination of sketchy knowledge, the enduring power of the Spartan mirage, and Sparta having been appropriated by others for rather murky ends. The inaccuracies of later writers can be best seen in a wonderful illustrated manuscript of the 36,365-line *Fall of Princes* by the English poet John Lydgate (*c.*1370–1451), which depicts Leonidas, King of Athens (!), as a knight in shining armour routing Persian knights, and an exhausted Xerxes, who fled from the battlefield, drinking from a river filled with the blood of slain Persians. Leonidas' *victory* at Thermopylae leads to a further scene depicting the humiliated Xerxes being dispatched by his own men.

The enduring power of the Spartan mirage can be seen in Rousseau's advocacy of a 'Legislator' who will be an 'extraordinary man' in his *Contrat social* (1762)—a none too subtle reference to Lycurgus—and the Abbé Mably's characterization of Sparta as a lost idyll where men were immune to the dangers of corruption because they were 'always occupied' by hunting, boxing, and wrestling. Heavily influenced by the likes of Rousseau and Mably, the leading French Revolutionary Robespierre (1758–94) believed that the new French Republic should regenerate mankind as Lycurgus had done at Sparta, writing: 'Sparta shines like a lightning-flash amid vast darknesses'. Saint-Just (1745–94) went one step further than Robespierre by actively advocating Lycurgan-style land-sharing after the overthrow of the monarchy. Neither survived to bring their Spartan desires to fruition.

The dark ends to which admiration of Sparta can lead are best seen in Nazi Germany where Spartophilia was linked to official policy. Bernhard Rust, the Reich Minister for

Education, stated in 1933: 'there is no doubt in my mind that we must rear a race of Spartans, and that those who are not prepared to join this community of Spartiates, must, as a result, relinquish any hope of being a citizen'. Adolf Hitler's praise of Sparta's 'naked aggression' became enshrined in official policy for the planned conquest of Eastern Europe. In 1942 Helmut Schubert, the head of the Commissariat for the Consolidation of the German Nation, wrote ominously that whereas the Germans would have Spartiate status, 'the Latvians, the Estonians and the like would be *perioikoi*, with the Russians as the helots'.

Official Nazi admiration of Sparta was even incorporated into the German education system, with the prominent German Classicist Helmut Berve (1896–1979) taking up the role of 'War-representative of German Classical Scholarship' (Kriegsbeauftrager der deutschen Altertumswissenschaft). Berve wrote a short monograph on Sparta in 1937, eulogizing the Spartans' heroism at Thermopylae, and stressing Sparta's links with Nazi Germany. Berve also gave lectures on Sparta to associations of soldiers, working men, and teachers, an early example of what universities today call 'public engagement'. Berve's vision of the Spartans was readily adopted by German school teachers and Classicists, with the syllabus at secondary and tertiary institutions altered to present the Spartans as 'Nordic culture-bearing peoples', who were part of the Germanic bloodline.

Berve also helped draft the curriculum at the 'Adolf-Hitler Schulen', Spartan-style boarding schools for the most physically and racially sound German 12–18-year-olds. Graduates of these schools were expected to become obedient, militaristic, 'political soldiers', who would become the next generation of Nazi party leaders and military officers. To help facilitate this transformation Berve co-authored a textbook with the prominent Classical archaeologist Otto-Wilhelm von Vocano (1910–97) called *Sparta: Der Lebenskampfe einer nordischen Herrenschicht* (*Sparta: The Life-Struggle of a Nordic Master-Caste*), which included chapters on Thermopylae, Spartan warfare, long quotations from Plutarch, Herodotus, and Thucydides, and a whole chapter of Tyrtaeus' war poetry (what Berve called an 'education for death'), printed double-spaced in a large font. Ultimately Berve's 'Nazification' of the Spartans so tainted the subject that it was not until 1983 that a professional German writer produced a history of Sparta, and only in the 1990s did German-speaking academics begin to treat the Spartans as a mainstream subject again.

The ugly side of the modern veneration of the Spartans can be seen in Greece today where the far-right political party Golden Dawn (*Chrysi Avgi*) see themselves as the inheritors of the Spartan tradition. The party's hymn runs: 'Trackers of ancient glories, Sons of brilliant struggles, We are the New Spartans'. A Golden Dawn member of the Greek parliament reportedly stated at the party's annual torch-lit celebration of the Battle of Thermopylae in July 2008: 'we are Sparta's shield, patiently guarding the body of Greece . . . We are waiting for the moment of a great counter attack, following in the steps of the ancient "Krypteia", who soundlessly killed the city's internal enemies in complete darkness and silence'. Unsurprisingly, Golden Dawn's opponents accuse them of exploiting Sparta to advocate violence against migrants to Greece, which is ironic, for if the Spartans really were the Dorian incomers they claimed to be, Golden Dawn Sparta enthusiasts are identifying themselves with outside invaders rather than the indigenous population.

Spartans in Modern Popular Culture: 'This is Sparta!'

The Spartans have had a strong impact on many aspects of modern popular culture, but it is almost impossible not to start with the blockbuster film *300* (2006) based loosely on the story of the Battle of Thermopylae (see Figure 13). Directed by Zack Snyder, and starring Gerard Butler as Leonidas, Lena Headey as Gorgo, and Michael Fassbender as the fictional Spartan warrior Stelios, *300* grossed $450 million at the box office. The scene in which Gerard Butler shouts 'This is Sparta!' before kicking Xerxes' jewel-covered envoy down a well is the first thing that many people today think of when they hear the name Sparta, and has spawned thousands of internet memes.

The Spartans of *300* are cartoonish, which is unsurprising given that Snyder has subsequently directed five DC Comic superhero films, and *300* is an adaptation of Frank Miller's 1998 graphic novel of the same name. Released in five separate issues in 1998 with the appropriately Spartan titles: 'Honor', 'Duty', 'Glory', 'Combat', and 'Victory', Miller's *300* was unashamedly epic, boasting high-quality paper and costly double-page 'splashes' illustrated by Miller's wife Lynn Varley. Snyder chose to film *300* using Chroma key compositing (the so-called 'blue screen') so that Varley's visual style could be reproduced on screen. Miller's work

Figure 13 Poster from the film *300* (2006), Warner Bros. Pictures.

itself was heavily influenced by Rudolph Maté's 'swords and sandals' epic, *The Three Hundred Spartans* (1962), starring Richard Egan as Leonidas. Ironically, two years earlier Egan had played the role of Ahasuerus, a.k.a. Xerxes, in the film *Esther and the King*. Miller has stated that seeing *The Three Hundred Spartans* changed the course of his creative life.

Both versions of *300* include frequent soundbites about Sparta that have some historical legitimacy, for example Dieneces' famous line 'we'll fight in the shade' is given to Stelios, and Leonidas tells his men 'tonight we dine in Hell', similar to Diodorus' version. But much of the film is fantasy, such as the bare-chested, leather-trunk-wearing Spartan warriors, and the portrayal of the ephors as 'diseased old mystics'. Worse still is the portrayal of Ephialtes as a bizarrely misshapen hunchback whose parents fled from Sparta to safeguard him against Spartan exposure of the disabled. Of the rampaging war rhinoceros in the film, I probably need say no more!

Both film and graphic novel have been criticized for lazy racism, such as the portrayal of Xerxes (played by Rodrigo Santoro in the film) as a bejewelled, half-naked, shaven-headed giant, who tries to flirt with Leonidas, or the portrayal of Hydarnes' Immortals as shiny-mask-wearing razor-toothed ninjas (a rather odd borrowing from Miller's earlier Marvel Comics *Elektra* series). But it is the portrayal of the Persians as freedom-hating bloodthirsty tyrants—Miller's graphic novel describes the Persians as 'poised to crush Greece, an island of reason and freedom in a sea of mysticism and tyranny'—that has most earned the wrath of critics in the West and the Middle East. *Slate* magazine even compared *300* to the notorious Nazi propaganda film *The Eternal Jew* as an extreme example of how 'race-baiting fantasy and nationalist myth can serve as an incitement to total war'.

But we need to remember that *300* is about entertainment. After all, Snyder's previous film was the 2004 remake of the zombie classic *Dawn of the Dead*, and Miller is probably best known for the neo-noir graphical novel (1991–2) and film (2005) *Sin City*. We can see the impact of the need to please an audience in the complete omission of the helots, and the transformation of Thermopylae's sole survivor, Aristodemus, into an atypically wordy Spartan storyteller sent home so that he can inspire the Spartans with a story 'that will burn in the hearts of free men for all the centuries yet to be'. Whereas Aristodemus rejected the chance to fight on that fateful last day because of his unknown eye disease, *300*'s Dilios wants to fight on despite having lost an eye—a wound that Leonidas dismisses as a 'scratch', prompting Dilios to agree, thanking the gods for gracing him with a 'spare'. Both the novel and the film end with Dilios inspiring 'ten thousand Spartans commanding thirty thousand free Greeks' to victory at Plataea. Snyder said using Dilios to tell the story allowed the introduction of a fantasy element to the story, noting 'Dilios is a guy who knows how not to wreck a good story with truth'. We should also remember that it is not just Miller and Snyder who portray Xerxes as an erratically-behaved tyrant who intended to enslave Greece—Herodotus and later Greek writers did the same.

The Spartans have also been the subject of numerous popular novels, most notably Steven Pressfield's *Gates of*

Fire (1998), which has sold more than one million copies worldwide. Pressfield's novel tells the story of Thermopylae from the perspective of Xeones, a young Acarnanian refugee, who describes himself as having been brought up as 'a sort of sparring partner for the youths enrolled in the agoge'. Xeones, who serves as a batman to the Spartiate Dieneces at Thermopylae, so hero-worships the Spartans that he is deemed 'more Spartan than the Spartans'. Xeones even spurns an offer of freedom to don hoplite armour and fight with Leonidas and his men in their fatal final stand.

Pressfield's Spartans closely resemble modern servicemen. There is even a Spartan version of the 'Rifleman's Creed' ('This is my rifle...'), with every Spartan taught to recite 'This is my shield, I bear it before me in battle, but it is not mine alone. It protects my brother on my left. It protects my city. I will never let my brother out of its shadow nor my city out of its shelter. I will die with my shield before me facing the enemy.' No wonder then that *Gates of Fire* is a set text at the US Marine Corps Basic School at Quantico, the United States Naval Academy, and West Point.

Older readers might remember *Black Sparta* (1928), a collection of short stories by the Scottish writer Naomi Mitchison (1887–1989). Mitchison wrote more than seventy books, and is perhaps best known for the historical/fantasy novel *The Corn King and the Spring Queen* (1931). Amongst the thirteen stories in *Black Sparta* (1928), three focus on the Spartans. 'Krypteia' tells the story of the Spartan youth Geranor's brutal killing of a helot goatherd, and the even more appalling execution of the helot's young son. 'The Lamb Misused' tells how a handsome blond Spartiate Melyllias

(a favourite of King Archidamus) and his half-brother
Telestas (implicitly a bastard son by a helot mother) escape
from captivity on Mt Ithome with the help of a helot girl,
Arné, after she falls in love with Melyllias. Although he
promises to marry Arné, Melyllias cold-heartedly marries
her off to a helot recommended by Archidamus. The longest
story, 'Black Sparta', centres on Tragon, a helot who escapes
from the pursing members of the *krypteia* with the help of
his childhood friend, the Spartiate Phylleidas.

The graphic novel *Three* by the British writer Kieron Gillen
(illustrated by Ryan Kelly, and coloured by Jordie Bellaire),
goes one step further in making the underdogs of Sparta
the heroes. *Three* tells the story of three fugitive helots—
the strong, but lame Klaros (later revealed to be short for
'Stenyklaros' where the rebellious helots wiped out 300 Spartans in the 460s BCE), his lover Damar, and the scrawny,
smart-mouthed, 'town helot' Terpander—who are being
pursued by 300 Spartiates for having murdered a small party
of Spartiates who had tried to kill them. Gillen's work deliberately mocks the Spartans, who need to send 300 fully-armed
warriors to pursue just three runaway slaves, and ultimately
have to resort to un-Spartan machinations to dislodge Klaros
from the cave-mouth he blocks while wearing armour he took
from a Spartiate he slew. Gillen's work also purposely echoes
that of Miller, even going so far as to offer what he calls 'ironic
intertexts', both visual and in the storyline. In preparing his
novel Gillen familiarized himself with modern scholarship on
Sparta, and *Three* even includes the text of a conversation
between Gillen and the eminent historian Professor Steve
Hodkinson, along with additional 'historical footnotes'

written by Gillen himself. Whereas our primary sources largely overlooked the helots, Mitchison and Gillen have succeeded in giving them names, voices, and even faces.

Modern Sporting Spartans

Sporting teams around the globe have long invoked the Spartan legend to promote team spirit, such as the Czech soccer team AC Sparta Prague (founded 1893), who have won the Czech top flight thirty-three times, or the Barbadian Sparta Cricket Club (founded 1893), whose most notable former players include Sir Clyde Walcott and the legendary fast bowler Sir Wes Hall. Some eleven North American colleges have teams known as 'the Spartans', with the most famous being the varsity teams of Michigan State University, who have been known as the 'Spartans' since 1926. MSU's football team are supported by the mascot 'Sparty' (Figure 14), an absurdly muscular stylized Greek hoplite with a prominent jutting chin, ironically sporting not a Greek hoplite's helmet, but an Imperial Roman legionary's helmet. Sparty even has his own Twitter feed and Wikipedia page. There are also countless high school teams in the US called 'the Spartans', my personal favourite being the 'Sparta Spartans' from the town of Sparta in Michigan, whose logo is a blue cartoonish Corinthian-style hoplite helmet, with a home address of 'Sparta Drive'—all in all about as Spartan as you can get. Even modern-day Sparta (Sparti) has got into the act, with the Athletic Union of Sparta Football Club founded in 1991. Currently playing in the Greek second division, their club crest bears the motto

Figure 14 'Sparty', the Michigan State University mascot (2007).

Η ΤΑΝ Η ΕΠΙ ΤΗΣ ('With it or on it'), and their most fanatical supporters are known as the '300'.

The Spartans are also invoked in modern endurance races, such as the annual (since 1983) 246 km ultramarathon race between Athens and Sparti called the 'Spartathlon', which commemorates Pheidippides the Athenian's run all the way from Athens to Sparta to beg for their help at the Battle of Marathon (490 BCE). The finishing point is a statue of Leonidas placed at the end of the main street of Sparti. There is also the endurance race known as the 'Spartan race', first held in 2010 in Williston Vermont, with competitors having to 'run, crawl, jump, and swim' and overcome a series of obstacles. Since 2013 the event has been televised, and there is now even a twice annual fully immersive training programme called the 'Agoge'. Since its inception the Spartan Race has been franchised to thirty countries around the globe, and spawned the NBC television series *Spartan: Ultimate Team Challenge* (2016–), and an Australian version, *Australian Spartan* (2018–).

The Spartan legacy

It is likely that the Spartans would be underwhelmed by their modern legacy of blood and gore films made simply for entertainment, football team mascots, and comic books about helots. I suspect they would have recognized a far more fitting tribute to their way of life in the poem *Thermopylae* (1910), by the Alexandrian Greek poet Constantine P. Cavafy (1863–1933), which (as translated by Edmund Keeley and Philip Sherrard) opens with the lines 'Honor to those who in the life they lead, define and guard a Thermopylae. Never betraying what is right'. And I am sure Cavafy's fatalistic final lines, 'and even more honor is due to them when they foresee (and many do foresee) that Ephialtis will turn up in the end, that the Medes will break through after all', would have appealed to Leonidas, who when asked what sort of a poet Tyrtaeus was, replied that he was good for encouraging young men to get themselves killed.

TIMELINE OF KEY EVENTS IN THE HISTORY OF THE SPARTANS

*c.*1000	Mythical 'Dorian' settlement of Sparta
*c.*900	Traditional date for Lycurgus as lawgiver at Sparta
776	Lycurgus helps hold first Olympic Games while lawgiver at Sparta (alternative traditional date for Lycurgus)
720	Acanthus the Spartan 'invents' naked running at the Olympic Games
*c.*700	Sparta conquers Messenia
676	Carneia festival founded at Sparta
669	Sparta defeated by Argos at Battle of Hysiae
*c.*650	Messenian revolt; *floruit* of Tyrtaeus
630	*floruit* of Alcman
*c.*570	'Battle of the Fetters' between Sparta and Tegea
556	Chilon ephor at Sparta
*c.*550	Sparta becomes allies with Tegea and other Peloponnesian *poleis*; Gitiadas adorns temple of Athena Chalkioikos; Bathycles dedicates throne of Apollo-Hyacinthus at Amyclae; Cyrus the Great founds Persian Empire
*c.*545	Sparta seizes Thyreatis from Argos; 'Battle of the Champions' between Sparta and Argos
525	Spartan expedition to Samos
*c.*520	Cleomenes becomes Agiad king

c.515	Demaratus becomes Eurypontid king
512	Anchimol(i)us leads unsuccessful Spartan attempt to end Hippias' tyranny at Athens
510	Cleomenes expels Hippias from Athens
508	Cleomenes invades Athens in failed attempt to install Isagoras as tyrant
506	Cleomenes leads unsuccessful invasion of Athens
504	Sparta's Peloponnesian allies refuse to help Spartans reinstall Hippias as tyrant at Athens
504?	Demaratus wins chariot race at Olympic Games
499	Aristagoras of Miletus visits Sparta
c.494	Cleomenes defeats Argives at Battle of Sepeia
491	Demaratus deposed; Leotychides becomes Eurypontid king
490	Battle of Marathon; Messenian helot revolt?; death of Cleomenes; accession of Leonidas as Agiad king
481	Spartans chosen to lead the war against Xerxes
480	Battle of Thermopylae (August); Battle of Salamis (September)
479	Battle of Plataea; Battle of Mycale
478	Pausanias the Spartan Regent leads allied campaign to liberate Cyprus and Byzantium from Persian rule; Pausanias recalled to Sparta due to misconduct
477	Ionian Greeks reject Pausanias' replacement Dorcis, and join Athenian-led Delian League
476?	Leotychides invades Thessaly, is caught taking bribes, and deposed
475	Debate at Sparta about fighting Athens for hegemony of the Greeks
470s	Defection of Tegea—Spartans fight alone against Tegeans and Argives
470	Pausanias again recalled to Sparta, and dies after seeking sanctuary in temple of Athena

464	Major earthquake strikes Laconia; Messenian helot revolt commences; 300 Spartans killed at Stenyclerus
462	Sparta appeals to Athens for help against Messenian rebels at Ithome
461	Sparta sends the Athenians home, ending friendly relations between the two cities
Late 460s	Spartans fight alone against the Arcadians at the Battle of Dipaea
457	Spartans and their Peloponnesian allies defeat the Athenians at the Battle of Tanagra
454	Messenians at Ithome surrender
445	Spartans invade Athens; Pleistoanax deposed as Agiad king after being bribed to withdraw; Thirty years' Peace agreed between the Spartans and the Athenians
c.440	Remains of Leonidas returned to Sparta
431	Outbreak of Peloponnesian war between the Spartans and their allies and Athens
427	Death of Archidamus II; accession of Agis II as Eurypontid king; return of Pleistoanax as Agiad king
425	Disaster at Sphacteria when 120 Spartan hoplites surrender to the Athenians
424	Brasidas begins campaigning against the Athenians in Thrace; Thucydides banished from Athens
422	Brasidas and the Athenian general Cleon are killed at Amphipolis
421	Peace of Nicias between Sparta and Athens and their respective allies; 50-year alliance between Sparta and Athens
420	Alliance between Athens, Argos, Elis, and Mantinea against Sparta; Eleans expel Spartans from the Olympic Games; Lichas the Spartan flogged at Olympia after attempting to claim the prize after winning the chariot race

418	Spartan victory at Battle of Mantinea
415	Athenian expedition to Sicily; Alcibiades defects to Sparta
414	Gylippus advises the Sicilians in the war against Athens
413	Sparta invades Athens and occupies Deceleia
412	Alcibiades leaves Sparta after alleged affair with Timagora, the wife of Agis II
411	Spartan alliance with Persia against Athens
410	Alcibiades defeats Spartan fleet at Cyzicus
406	Lysander defeats Athenian fleet at Notium; Callicratidas defeated by Athenian fleet at Battle of Arginusae
405	Lysander destroys Athenian fleet in Battle of Aegospotami
404	Athens surrenders to Sparta ending the Peloponnesian war; Spartans set up puppet government of 'Thirty Tyrants' at Athens, including Critias; Lysander accorded divine honours at Samos
403	Sparta intervenes in Athenian civil war; Spartan deceased including Chaeron and Thibrachus buried in Kerameikos; restoration of Athenian democracy
402	Spartans aid Cyrus the Younger in his failed attempt to overthrow his brother Artaxerxes and claim the throne of Persia
401	Cyrus defeated at Battle of Cunaxa
400	Spartans subdue Elis and are permitted to compete at the Olympic Games; Agesilaus succeeds Agis II as Eurypontid king
399	Conspiracy of Cinadon; Sparta declares war on Persia
396	Agesilaus invades Asia; Cynisca wins four-horse chariot race at the Olympic Games
395	Thebes, Athens, Argos, and Corinth launch Corinthian war against Sparta; Lysander killed at Haliartus; Pausanias deposed as Agiad king

394	Agesilaus recalled from Asia; Spartan fleet destroyed at Battle of Cnidus; Spartan victories on land at Nemea River and Coronea
392	Cynisca wins four-horse chariot race at the Olympic Games for second time
390	Entire *mora* of Spartan army wiped out in fighting near Corinth
387	'King's Peace' ends Corinthian War and secures Spartan hegemony in Greece
385	Sparta breaks up former ally Mantinea into villages
382	Sparta installs garrison at Thebes
379	Sparta reduces Phleius and Olynthus; Thebes expels Spartan garrison
378	Sparta makes abortive raid on Athenian port of Piraeus; Athens founds anti-Spartan alliance
375	Thebans defeat Spartans at Battle of Tegyra
371	Thebans defeat Spartans at the Battle of Leuctra; end of Spartan hegemony in Greece
370	Theban invasion of Laconia; 6,000 helots accept offer of freedom to fight with the Spartans; Epaminondas the Theban liberates the Messenians and founds new Messenian *polis*

REFERENCES

CHAPTER 1: GO TELL THE SPARTANS

Ernle Bradford, *Thermopylae: The Battle for the West* (Cambridge, MA: Da Capo Press, 2004).

Paul Cartledge, 'The Birth of the Hoplite: Sparta's Contribution to Early Greek Military Organization', in *Spartan Reflections*, 153–66 (London: Duckworth, 2001).

Paul Cartledge, 'What Have the Spartans Done for Us? Sparta's Contribution to Western Civilisation', *Greece & Rome*, 51 (2004), 164–79.

Paul Cartledge, *Thermopylae: The Battle that Changed the World* (London: Pam Macmillan, 2006).

Peter Green, *The Greco-Persian Wars* (Berkeley: University of California Press, 1996).

Nicholas G. L. Hammond, 'Sparta at Thermopylae', *Historia*, 45 (1996): 1–20.

Noreen Humble, 'Why the Spartans Fight So Well...Even in Disorder—Xenophon's View', in *Sparta & War*, eds. S. Hodkinson and A. Powell, 219–34 (Swansea: Classical Press of Wales, 2006).

J. F. Lazenby, *The Spartan Army* (Barnsley: Pen & Sword Military, 2012).

Nicole Loraux, 'The Spartans' "Beautiful Death"', in *The Experiences of Tiresias: The Feminine and the Greek Man*, 77–91 (Princeton: Princeton University Press, 1995).

Marcello Lupi, 'Sparta and the Persian Wars, 499–478', in *A Companion to Sparta*, ed. A. Powell, 271–90 (Malden, MA: Wiley Blackwell, 2017).

Anton Powell, 'Sparta's Foreign—and Internal—History 478–403', in *A Companion to Sparta*, ed. A. Powell, 291–319 (Malden, MA: Wiley Blackwell, 2017).

Françoise Ruzé, 'The Empire of the Spartans (404–371)', in *A Companion to Sparta*, ed. A. Powell, 320–53 (Malden, MA: Wiley Blackwell, 2017).

CHAPTER 2: SPARTA'S CIVIC STRUCTURE

Paul Cartledge, 'The Spartan Kingship: Doubly Odd', in *Spartan Reflections*, 55–67 (London: Duckworth, 2001).

Paul Cartledge, *Sparta and Lakonia: A Regional History, 1300–362 B.C.*, 2nd edition (London and New York: Routledge, 2002).

William G. Cavanagh, 'An Archaeology of Ancient Sparta with Reference to Laconia and Messenia', in *A Companion to Sparta*, ed. A. Powell, 61–92 (Malden, MA: Wiley Blackwell, 2017).

Jean Ducat, 'The Spartan "Tremblers"', in *Sparta & War*, eds. S. Hodkinson and A. Powell, 1–56 (Swansea: Classical Press of Wales, 2006).

Jean Ducat, 'The Perioikoi', in *A Companion to Sparta*, ed. A. Powell, 596–614 (Malden, MA: Wiley Blackwell, 2017).

Michael Lipka, *Xenophon's* Spartan Constitution*: Introduction, Text, Commentary* (Berlin, 2002).

Ellen G. Millender, 'Kingship: The History, Power, and Prerogatives of the Spartans' "Divine" Dyarchy', in *A Companion to Sparta*, ed. A. Powell, 452–79 (Malden, MA: Wiley Blackwell, 2017).

Massimo Nafissi, 'Lykourgos the Spartan "Lawgiver": Ancient Beliefs and Modern Scholarship', in *A Companion to Sparta*, ed. A. Powell, 93–123 (Malden, MA: Wiley Blackwell, 2017).

CHAPTER 3: THE SPARTAN LIFESTYLE

Alfred S. Bradford, 'The Duplicitous Spartan', in *Shadow of Sparta*, eds. A. Powell and S. Hodkinson, 59–85 (London: Routledge, 1994).

Paul Christesen, 'Sparta and Athletics', in *A Companion to Sparta*, ed. A. Powell, 543–64 (Malden, MA: Wiley Blackwell, 2017).

Ephraim David, 'Sparta and the Politics of Nudity', in *Sparta: The Body Politic*, eds. A. Powell and S. Hodkinson, 137–63 (Swansea: Classical Press of Wales, 2010).

Thomas J. Figueira, 'The Nature of the Spartan Kleros', in *Spartan Society*, ed. T. J. Figueira, 47–76 (Swansea: Classical Press of Wales, 2004).

Thomas J. Figueira, 'Xenelasia and Social Control in Classical Sparta', *Classical Quarterly*, 53 (2003): 44–74.

N. R. E. Fisher, 'Drink, *Hybris* and the Promotion of Harmony in Sparta', in *Classical Sparta: Techniques Behind Her Success*, ed. A. Powell, 26–50 (London: Routledge, 1989).

Mogens H. Hansen, 'Was Sparta a Normal or Exceptional Polis?', in *Sparta: Comparative Approaches*, ed. S. Hodkinson, 385–416 (Swansea: Classical Press of Wales, 2009).

Mogens H. Hansen and Stephen Hodkinson, 'Spartan Exceptionalism? Continuing the Debate', in *Sparta: Comparative Approaches*, ed. S. Hodkinson, 473–98 (Swansea: Classical Press of Wales, 2009).

Stephen Hodkinson, *Property and Wealth in Classical Sparta* (Swansea: Classical Press of Wales, 2000).

Stephen Hodkinson, 'Was Classical Sparta a Military Society?' in *Sparta & War*, eds. S. Hodkinson and A. Powell, 111–62 (Swansea: Classical Press of Wales, 2006).

Stephen Hodkinson, 'Was Sparta an Exceptional Polis?', in *Sparta: Comparative Approaches*, ed. S. Hodkinson, 417–72 (Swansea: Classical Press of Wales, 2009).

Stephen Hodkinson, 'Sparta: An Exceptional Domination of State over Society?', in *A Companion to Sparta*, ed. A. Powell, 29–58 (Malden, MA: Wiley Blackwell, 2017).

Polly Low, 'Commemorating the Spartan War-Dead', in *Sparta & War*, eds. S. Hodkinson and A. Powell, 85–109 (Swansea: Classical Press of Wales, 2004).

Michael Pettersson, *Cults of Apollo at Sparta: The Hyakinthia, the Gymnopaidiai and the Karneia* (Stockholm: Svenska institutet i Athen, 1992).

Anton Powell, 'Sparta: Reconstructing History from Secrecy, Lies and Myth', in *A Companion to Sparta*, ed. A. Powell, 3–28 (Malden, MA: Wiley Blackwell, 2017).

Nicolas Richer, 'The Religious System at Sparta', in *A Companion to Greek Religion*, ed. D. Ogden, 236–52 (Malden, MA: Wiley Blackwell, 2010).

Hans van Wees, 'Luxury, Austerity and Equality in Sparta', in *A Companion to Sparta*, ed. A. Powell, 202–35 (Malden, MA: Wiley Blackwell, 2017).

CHAPTER 4: RAISING A SPARTAN

Paul Cartledge, 'A Spartan Education', in *Spartan Reflections*, 79–90 (London: Duckworth, 2001).

James Davidson, *The Greeks and Greek Love: A Radical Reappraisal of Homosexuality in Ancient Greece* (London: Weidenfeld & Nicolson, 2007).

Jean Ducat, *Spartan Education: Youth and Society in the Classical Period* (Swansea: Classical Press of Wales, 2006).

Thomas J. Figueira, 'The Spartan *Hippeis*', in *Sparta & War*, eds. S. Hodkinson and A. Powell, 57–84 (Swansea: Classical Press of Wales, 2004).

Nigel Kennell, *The Gymnasium of Virtue: Education & Culture in Ancient Sparta* (Chapel Hill: University of North Carolina Press, 1995).

Ellen Millender, 'Spartan Literacy Revisited', *Classical Antiquity*, 20 (2001): 121–64.

Anton Powell, 'Spartan Education', in *A Companion to Ancient Education*, ed. W.M. Bloomer, 90–111 (Malden, MA: Wiley Blackwell, 2015).

Nicolas Richer, 'Spartan Education in the Classical Period', in *A Companion to Sparta*, ed. A. Powell, 524–42 (Malden, MA: Wiley Blackwell, 2017).

CHAPTER 5: SPARTAN WOMEN

Paul Cartledge, 'Spartan Wives: Liberation or Licence?', *Classical Quarterly*, 31 (1981): 84–105.

M. Dillon, 2007. 'Were Spartan Women Who Died in Childbirth Honoured with Grave Inscriptions?', *Hermes*, 135 (2007): 149–65.

Thomas J. Figueira, 'Gynecocracy: How Women Policed Masculine Behavior in Archaic and Classical Sparta', in *Sparta: The Body Politic*, eds. A. Powell and S. Hodkinson, 265–96 (Swansea: Classical Press of Wales, 2010).

Stephen Hodkinson, 'Female Property Ownership and Empowerment in Classical and Hellenistic Sparta', in *Spartan Society*, ed. T. J. Figueira, 103–36 (Swansea: Classical Press of Wales, 2004).

Ellen Millender 'Spartan Women', in *A Companion to Sparta*, ed. A. Powell, 500–24 (Malden, MA: Wiley Blackwell, 2017).

Sarah B. Pomeroy, *Spartan Women* (New York: Oxford University Press, 2002).

Anton Powell, 'The Women of Sparta—and of Other Greek Cities—at War', in *Spartan Society*, ed. T. J. Figueira, 137–50 (Swansea: Classical Press of Wales, 2004).

Andrew G. Scott, 'Plural Marriages and the Spartan State', *Historia*, 60 (2011): 413–24.

CHAPTER 6: HELOTS

Paul Cartledge, 'Richard Talbert's Revision of the Sparta-Helot Struggle: A Reply', *Historia*, 40: (1991), 379–81.

Paul Cartledge, 'Raising Hell? The Helot Mirage—A Personal Re-View', in *Helots and Their Masters in Laconia and Messenia: Histories, Ideologies, Structures*, eds. Nino Luraghi and Susan E. Alcock, 12–30 (Cambridge, MA: Harvard University Press, 2003)

Thomas Figueira, 'Helotage and the Spartan Economy', in *A Companion to Sparta*, ed. A. Powell, 565–95 (Malden, MA: Wiley Blackwell, 2017).

David Harvey, 'The Clandestine Massacre of the Helots (Thucydides 4.80)', in *Spartan Society*, ed. T. J. Figueira, 199–217 (Swansea: Classical Press of Wales, 2004).

David Lewis, *Greek Slave Systems in their Eastern Mediterranean Context, c.800–146 BC* (Oxford: Oxford University Press, 2018).

Stefan Link, 'Snatching and Keeping: The Motif of Taking in Spartan Culture', in *Spartan Society*, ed. T. J. Figueira, 1–24 (Swansea: Classical Press of Wales, 2004).

Nino Luraghi, 'The Imaginary Conquest of the Helots', in *Helots and Their Masters in Laconia and Messenia: Histories, Ideologies, Structures*, eds. Nino Luraghi and Susan E. Alcock, 109–41 (Cambridge, MA: Harvard University Press, 2003).

Nino Luraghi, *The Ancient Messenians* (Cambridge: Cambridge University Press, 2008).

Nino Luraghi, 'The Helots: Comparative Approaches, Ancient and Modern', in *Sparta: Comparative Approaches*, ed. S. Hodkinson, 261–304 (Swansea: Classical Press of Wales, 2009).

Ellen Millender, 'Spartan State Terror: Violence, Humiliation, and the Reinforcement of Social Boundaries', in *Brill's Companion to Insurgency and Terrorism in the Ancient Mediterranean*, eds. Timothy Howe and Lee L. Brice, 117–50 (Leiden: Brill, 2016).

Annalisa Paradiso, 'The Logic of Terror: Thucydides, Spartan Duplicity and an Improbable Massacre', in *Spartan Society*, ed. T. J. Figueira, 179–98 (Swansea: Classical Press of Wales, 2004).

Richard J. A. Talbert, 'The Role of the Helots in the Class Struggle at Sparta', *Historia*, 38 (1989): 22–40.

Hans van Wees, 'Conquerors and Serfs: Wars of Conquest and Forced Labour in Archaic Greece', in *Helots and Their Masters in Laconia and Messenia: Histories, Ideologies, Structures*, eds. Nino Luraghi and Susan E. Alcock, 33–80 (Cambridge, MA: Harvard University Press, 2003).

CHAPTER 7: THE LATER RECEPTION OF SPARTA

Lynn S. Fotheringham, 'The Positive Portrayal of Sparta in Late-Twentieth-Century Fiction', in *Sparta in Modern Thought: Politics, History and Culture*, eds. S. Hodkinson and I. Macgregor Morris, 393–428 (Swansea: Classical Press of Wales, 2012).

Kieron Gillen, *Three* (Portland, OR: Image Comics, 2014).

Sean R. Jensen, 'Reception of Sparta in North America: Eighteenth to Twenty-First Centuries', in *A Companion to Sparta*, ed. A. Powell, 704–22 (Malden, MA: Wiley Blackwell, 2017).

Haydn Mason, 'Sparta in the French Enlightenment', in *Sparta in Modern Thought: Politics, History and Culture*, eds. S. Hodkinson and I. Macgregor Morris, 71–104 (Swansea: Classical Press of Wales, 2012).

References

Frank Miller, *300* (Milwaukee, OR: Darkhorse Books, 1999).

Ian Macgregor Morris, 'The Paradigm of Democracy: Sparta in Enlightenment Thought', in *Spartan Society*, ed. T. J. Figueira, 339–62 (Swansea: Classical Press of Wales, 2004).

Gideon Nisbet, *Ancient Greece in Film and Popular Culture*, 2nd edition (Bristol: Bristol Phoenix Press, 2008).

Steven Pressfield, *Gates of Fire: An Epic Novel of the Battle of Thermopylae* (London: Bantam Books, 2000).

Elizabeth Rawson, *The Spartan Tradition in European Thought* (Oxford: Oxford University Press, 1969).

Stefan Rebenich, 'Reception of Sparta in Germany and German-Speaking Europe', in *A Companion to Sparta*, ed. A. Powell, 685–703 (Malden, MA: Wiley Blackwell, 2017).

Helen Roche, *Sparta's German Children* (Swansea: Classical Press of Wales, 2013).

FURTHER READING ON
THE SPARTANS

There has been a surge of work on Sparta in the last three decades, much of it generated by the International Sparta Seminar, to which I have had on occasion the privilege of contributing. The following is by no means a comprehensive reading list, but rather a mix of the most recent volumes devoted to Sparta and the Spartans, much of it generated by the Sparta Seminar series, and much of it necessarily in English.

Luis Filipe Bantim de Assumpção, ed., *Esparta. Política e sociedade* (Curitiba: Editora Prismas, 2017).

Paul Cartledge, *Agesilaos and the Crisis of Sparta* (London: Duckworth, 1987).

Paul Cartledge, *Spartan Reflections* (London: Duckworth, 2001).

Paul Cartledge, *Sparta and Lakonia: A Regional History, 1300–362 B.C.*, 2nd edition (Abingdon: Routledge, 2002).

Paul Cartledge and Antony Spawforth, *Hellenistic and Roman Sparta: A Tale of Two Cities* (London: Duckworth, 1989).

Paul Cartledge, Nikos Birgalias, and Kostas Buraselis, eds., *H συμβολή της αρχαίας Σπάρτης στην πολιτική σκέψη και πρακτική* (*The Contribution of Ancient Sparta to Political Thought and Practice*) (Athens: Alexandria Publications, 2007).

William G. Cavanagh and S. E. C. Walker, eds., *Sparta in Laconia: The Archaeology of a City in its Countryside. Proceedings of the 19th British Museum Colloquium* (London: British School at Athens, 1998).

William G. Cavanagh, Christopher Mee, and P. James, eds., *The Laconia Rural Sites Project, Annual of the British School at Athens*, Supplement 36 (London: British School at Athens, 2005).

Jacqueline Christien and Françoise Ruzé, *Sparte. Géographie, mythes et histoire* (Paris: Armand Colin, 2007).

M. G. L. Cooley, *LACTOR 21: Sparta* (London: London Association of Classical Teachers, 2017).

Thomas J. Figueira, ed., *Spartan Society* (Swansea: Classical Press of Wales, 2004).

L. F. Fitzhardinge, *The Spartans* (London: Thames & Hudson, 1980).

Stephen Hodkinson, *Property and Wealth in Classical Sparta* (Swansea: Classical Press of Wales, 2000).

Stephen Hodkinson, ed., *Sparta: Comparative Approaches* (Swansea: Classical Press of Wales, 2009).

Stephen Hodkinson and Ian Macgregor Morris, eds., *Sparta in Modern Thought: Politics, History and Culture* (Swansea: Classical Press of Wales, 2012).

Stephen Hodkinson and Anton Powell, eds., *Sparta: New Perspectives* (Swansea: Classical Press of Wales, 1999).

Stephen Hodkinson and Anton Powell, eds., *Sparta & War* (Swansea: Classical Press of Wales, 2006).

Nigel M. Kennell, *The Spartans* (Malden, MA: Wiley Blackwell, 2010).

Edmond Lévy, *Sparte. Histoire politique et sociale jusqu'à la conquête romaine* (Paris: Seuil, 2003).

Marcello Lupi, *L'Ordine delle generazioni. Classi di età e costumi matrimoniali nell'antica Sparta* (Bari: Edipuglia, 2000).

Andreas Luther, Mischa Meier, and Lukas Thommen, eds., *Das Frühe Sparta* (Stuttgart: Franz Steiner Verlag, 2006).

Massimo Nafissi, *La nascita del kosmos. Studi sulla storia e la società di Sparta* (Naples: Edizioni Scientifiche Italiane, 1991).

François Ollier, *Le mirage spartiate. Étude sur l'idéalisation de Sparte dans l'antiquité grecque,* 2 volumes (Paris 1933–43).

Vassiliki Pothou and Anton Powell, eds., *Das antike Sparta* (Stuttgart: Steiner Franz Verlag, 2017).

Anton Powell, ed., *Classical Sparta: Techniques behind Her Success* (London: Routledge, 1989).

Anton Powell, ed., *A Companion to Sparta* (Malden, MA: Wiley Blackwell, 2017).

Anton Powell and Stephen Hodkinson, eds., *Shadow of Sparta* (London: Routledge, 1994).

Anton Powell and Stephen Hodkinson, eds., *Sparta: Beyond the Mirage* (Swansea: Classical Press of Wales, 2002).

Anton Powell and Stephen Hodkinson, eds., *Sparta: The Body Politic* (Swansea: Classical Press of Wales, 2010).

Nicolas Richer, *Les éphores. Études sur l'histoire et sur l'image de Sparte (VIIIe–IIIe siècles avant Jésus-Christ)* (Paris: Publications de la Sorbonne, 1998).

Nicolas Richer, *La religion des Spartiates. Croyances et cultes dans l'Antiquité* (Paris: Belles lettres, 2012).

Nicolas Richer, *Sparte. Cité des arts, des armes et des lois* (Paris: Perrin, 2018).

Scott M. Rusch, *Sparta at War: Strategy, Tactics, and Campaigns, 550–362 BC* (Barnsley: Frontline Books, 2011).

Nick Sekunda, *The Spartan Army* (Oxford: Osprey Publishing, 1988).

Michael Whitby, ed., *Sparta* (Edinburgh: Edinburgh University Press, 2002).

INDEX

Agesilaus (Eurypontid king) 33, 47, 50–1, 57, 63, 65, 67, 86, 94, 107, 108

Agis II (Eurypontid king) 56, 65

Alcman (Spartan poet) 2, 42, 96, 124

Archidamus II (Eurypontid king) 94, 126, 143

Aristodemus 23–5, 33, 141

arms and armour 10–13, 15–16, 19, 21, 47, 78, 100, 109, 117, 142

Athens, Athenians 3, 13, 22, 33, 41, 50, 53–4, 61–2, 66, 67, 70–1, 72, 78, 84, 86, 99, 100, 101, 106, 117, 125, 126–7, 133, 135, 145

Battle of Mantinea (418 BCE) 37, 56, 64, 65

Battle of Plataea (479 BCE) 22–3, 24, 33, 37, 67, 116, 126

Battle of Stenyclarus (460s BCE) 126, 143

Battle of Thermopylae (480 BCE) 1–25, 30, 42, 43, 50, 52, 116, 135, 136, 137, 138–41, 142

'beautiful death' 20, 102

Brasidas 40, 86

burial practices 53–4, 102, 109

Cleomenes (Agiad king) 43, 60, 64, 68–9, 105, 113, 119

corporal punishment 71, 73, 77, 80, 81, 122

Cynisca 107–8

Demaratus (Eurypontid king) 7, 14, 36–7, 63–4, 69, 103–4, 119

dining practices 21, 28, 31, 48–9, 52–3, 54–60, 62, 78–9, 113, 122

dress 10, 28, 30–1, 32–3, 37, 53, 78, 80, 89, 122, 140

Elders (*gerousia*) 41, 43, 44

Ephialtes 18–9, 140, 146

ephors 29, 43, 44–5, 56, 57, 59, 62, 64, 65, 70, 71, 79, 84, 86, 87, 88, 91, 105–6, 119, 122, 127

facial hair 32–3, 45, 90, 92

female dress 96–7, 110

freed helots (*neodamodeis*) 40–1, 123–4

Gorgo 6, 64, 99, 100, 101, 105, 109, 138

Gylippus 32, 70–1

Index

hair 7, 8–10, 15, 31, 78, 90, 96, 103, 106
Helen of Troy (née Sparta) 61, 95, 103, 108
helots 1, 5, 22, 24, 26, 30, 32, 34, 38–40, 44–5, 49, 57, 59, 61, 68–9, 69–70, 78, 92, 93, 111–28, 131, 133, 136, 141, 142–4, 146; see also freed helots; Messenia, Messenians; rebellion by helots

'inferiors' (hypomeiones) 31–2, 114

Kaiadas 70, 74, 123
krypteia 91–2, 122, 127, 137, 143

Leonidas (Agiad king) 5–8, 12, 14, 16, 18–22, 23, 30, 35–6, 42–3, 50, 105–6, 109, 116, 130, 131, 132–3, 135, 138–41, 142, 145, 146
Lycurgus (mythical lawgiver) 4, 28–9
Lysander 32, 67, 70, 104

Menelaus (mythical king) 20, 61, 87
Messenia, Messenians 29–30, 38–40, 103, 111–13, 115, 119–22, 124, 126–8; see also helots; rebellion by helots

nudity 6–7, 15, 52, 63, 79, 95, 98–9, 131, 132–3, 135–6

Olympic Games 6, 52, 107–8
oracles 19, 41, 43, 69, 70, 121

paidonomos 76, 77, 91
Pantites 23–4
Pausanias (Spartan Regent) 37, 67, 69–70

Pausanias (Agiad king) 23, 85
Peloponnesian League 5, 65
perioikoi 26, 34–8, 40, 48, 93, 116, 125, 133, 136

rebellion by helots 39, 112–13, 118, 124–8, 143
religious practices 6, 19, 35, 48–9, 60–4, 70, 82–3; see also oracles

shame 1, 15, 24, 33, 93, 98, 103
Sosibius (Spartan historian) 2, 80
Spartan mirage 2–3, 4–5, 71–2, 134–5
sport, athletics, physical exercise 6–7, 15, 33, 46, 51–2, 82–3, 95–9, 135

Thebes, Thebans 20, 21, 31, 88, 110, 124, 125, 128
theft 70, 73, 80, 81, 83
300 (2006 film) 42–3, 109, 138–41
'tremblers' (tresantes) 24, 32–3, 92
Tyrtaeus (Spartan poet) 2, 13, 20, 39, 42, 114, 124–5, 137, 146

upbringing 28, 32, 37–8, 59, 71, 73–94, 142

women 32, 47, 63, 74, 89, 95–110, 116, 125; see also Cynisca; Gorgo

Xerxes 5–8, 13, 14, 15–7, 18, 20, 21–2, 23, 35–6, 42–3, 62, 69, 126, 127, 131, 135, 138, 140, 141